Women in Neighborhood Evangelism

Marjorie Stewart

Gospel Publishing House
Springfield, Missouri
02-0723

© Copyright 1978 by the Gospel Publishing House, Springfield, MO 65802. All rights reserved. No part of this book may be reproduced, stored in a retrieval system, or transmitted in any form or by any means, electronic, mechanical, photocopy, recording, or otherwise, without written permission of the copyright owner, except brief quotations used in connection with reviews in magazines or newspapers.

Library of Congress Catalog Card Number 77-93410
International Standard Book Number 0-88243-723-2
Printed in the United States of America

Preface

Books are never written by one person alone. The following are among those who enabled me to put in writing something of the joy and concept of neighborhood evangelism:

Alma Radford, who obeyed the Spirit's nudging to bring her neighbors together to hear God's Word.

Pastors Marcus Gaston, Charles Anderson, and Ed Weising, who all generously allowed me to develop this ministry as I felt God leading—graciously encouraging and counseling along the way.

Ruth Crawford, Northwest District Women's Ministries president, who became as excited as I about getting women to study God's Word.

Rev. Frank McAllister, Northwest District superintendent, and the District Presbytery who permitted me to tell the women of other churches about neighborhood evangelism.

Rev. Frank Cole and his wife Jean, who shared the excitement of their own revival in Port Angeles, Washington through a neighborhood Bible study program.

And, of course, all those wonderful women in many churches, but especially Calvary Temple, Seattle, who became involved and willingly shared their experiences with me.

Not least, nor last in importance, is the unique family God has blessed me with. They have been my greatest source of encouragement, carrying the burden right along with me for neighborhood evangelism.

I am also grateful to the *Pentecostal Evangel* for permission to adapt material that first appeared in its pages.

Contents

1 Open Doors 7
2 Neighbors in Need 13
3 Encounter With God 23
4 Alive and Active 33
5 Enabling of the Spirit 43
6 Are They Hearing What You're Asking? 51
7 Do They Know You Care? 63
8 The Bible Study and the Family 73
9 The Bible Study and the Church 79
10 Joy in Neighborhood Evangelism 89
11 How to Start a Neighborhood Bible Study 93

Looking at Jesus With Luke 105
Resource Materials 123

1
Open Doors

"This church stuff!" Mary said to the mother of her son's friend. "I don't want anyone to preach to me—but I wish I could go some place and just get some answers."

Without appearing the least bit shocked, Sonja answered, "I just happen to have a Tuesday morning Bible study. Would you be interested in coming?"

Mary came, and in a couple of weeks she responded to Jesus Christ, giving her heart and life to Him.

Many women like Sonja's friend are looking for answers to their muddled and conflict-ridden lives. Spiritual hunger is a fact of the 20th century, creating the harvest situation Jesus referred to in Matthew 9:37: "The harvest truly is plenteous, but the laborers are few."

Within the past dozen years we have seen a change in the attitudes of people toward religion. The atheistic-agnostic position is not as popular as it used to be. Anything with a tinge of the mystical, whether it be of God or the occult, captures attention.

As a result, the doors to many of our neighbors' homes are unlocked—just waiting for us to knock and walk in with the good news of God's love for them. Many of these women will not come to our churches, but they will accept an invitation to be a part of a neighborhood Bible-study group.

This has been my experience as I've led several small neighborhood groups in the greater Seattle area. I've helped other women start Bible studies in their neighborhoods and they too have found women who would come to their homes to discover what God's Word says.

Women across our nation are experiencing this response in their neighborhoods. A pastor's wife in Massachusetts reports that a young mother who felt she couldn't do much for the Lord opened her home to a Bible study. As a result, three women found eternal life in Jesus Christ.

From the other side of our country, in California, a volume of praise ascends to the Father weekly for the miraculous answers to prayer in groups of women who meet to study His Word and to care for each other. One of these women tells how through being invited to a Bible study she rededicated her life to Christ, received the baptism in the Holy Spirit, and returned to the church to stay.

Around the World

Small-group Bible studies have become international as the excitement is carried from one country to another. A woman in a group I attended some years ago moved to Germany and started a Bible study there because she had gained so much from our group in the United States.

In Hong Kong a missionary's wife tells of English-speaking Chinese women who meet weekly to study together. In the same city a group of expatriates from Australia share in a group.

Groups turn up everywhere, from South Africa to the Philippines and from Norway to Israel.

This movement is not new. Small-group ministries have been an important part of revival throughout church history. Jesus set the pattern almost 2000 years ago when He organized the first small group. He spent time with 12 men—eating, walking, and living with them. He taught them. He demonstrated His life-style and His power to change lives. He answered their questions. Then after sacrificing His own life, He told them to go and do for others what He had done for them.

In a similar way today, the Holy Spirit is calling people to come together in small groups to learn about Jesus.

It was early spring 1970 when a friend said to me, "Marj, would you be willing to lead a Bible study in my neighborhood?"

I was almost without an answer. Alma had no idea God was using her to fulfill a desire of my heart. I had participated in small-group Bible studies before and had seen people respond to the Word. It's like eating potato chips. One taste calls for another.

Fourteen curious women responded to our invitation that first Friday afternoon. For the next 4 years the group averaged from eight to twelve. Four of us were Assemblies of God women; the rest were from a variety of religious persuasions. One was a declared agnostic. Yet they all came week after week.

For 4 years we learned together what God is saying through His Word. We became acquainted with Jesus Christ in a more intimate way than we'd ever experienced before. We shared our burdens and our troubled hearts and also our joys. We prayed together. We prayed for each other. We cried and fasted for the ones who needed miracles in their lives. But, most of all, we searched God's Word together and put its truths down in our hearts.

During that period we saw God touch the lives of those women so they are not the same today. Some gave their lives to Him, some did not. Some came alive in Him and went on to win others to the Lord.

Guided by the Spirit

In the beginning of our neighborhood Bible study we weren't sure how to proceed. We learned by doing, but doing under the guidance of the Holy Spirit. Before we invited the first neighbor we held a prayer meeting. We asked God to guide our efforts. And as we look back on those 4 years of ministry in one of the most affluent neighborhoods in suburban Seattle, we are satisfied that God directed.

All of us learned of God in far greater measure than we ever would have guessed. From the start we determined to show the neighborhood that God's Word is alive and His love for them is real.

We thought we were putting God to the test. In reality we were putting our own commitment on the line. For 4 years, every Friday afternoon was closed to everything else. Nothing took precedence over the neighborhood Bible study. Doctor and dentist appointments were scheduled for other days; hair appointments were shuffled; the week's work was arranged around the Bible study.

For 4 years whenever one of the members needed help spiritually or physically, everything else was dropped and prayer was offered, many times along with tangible help. Days were set aside for fasting and prayer. Our social lives, including that of our husbands, revolved around the neighborhood Bible study group.

Has it been worth it? I believe it has. My own understanding of God and His Word has grown. And there were decisions for Christ which brought joy to our hearts and in heaven.

The desire to have you share the same joy has led to the writing of this book. The Psalmist wrote many centuries ago:

> They that sow in tears shall reap in joy. He that goeth forth and weepeth, bearing precious seed, shall doubtless come again with rejoicing, bringing his sheaves with him (Psalm 126:5, 6).

The seed, of course, is the Word of God. We are promised joy when we faithfully and prayerfully share His Word.

In the New Testament, Jesus said: "Joy shall be in heaven over one sinner that repenteth" (Luke 15:7).

Joy for you and joy in heaven! Yes, there is joy in neighborhood evangelism.

2

Neighbors in Need

An invitation to attend a Friday afternoon tea at Lois' home was phoned to every woman in the neighborhood. A special speaker was invited to tell her life story. Then we planned to share the idea of a Bible study in the neighborhood. When we invited the women we told them of our plans.

We had no idea who would want to come. We prayed the week preceding that the Lord would bring the ones He wanted there. When 14 women walked through the front door, we were overwhelmed with the response.

We knew we wanted to share the Word of God with these women. We knew we had been prompted by the Holy Spirit to give witness of God's love in that neighborhood. What we did not know were the oversized needs in the lives of some of those women—needs that only God himself could meet. Nor did we realize the Lord would make us instruments in His hands to meet those needs. Very honestly, if we had known at that time, we might have canceled everything! The job was a big one!

Behind some of those well-dressed women living in one of the most affluent suburbs of Seattle, were lives filled with heartaches. During the next few years we suffered, cried, and prayed together over a child needing open-heart surgery, over the mental breakdown of one of our members, over husbands who denied the truth, and over sons and daughters who needed God's deliverance from temptation.

Who Is My Neighbor?

We learned something of what Jesus meant in Luke 10:25-37 when He defined the term *neighbor* for an impudent lawyer.

The lawyer stood up in a public meeting, thinking he would put Jesus in His place. His question was not original; others had asked it too. In fact, sooner or later almost all of us ask it.

"Master, what shall I do to inherit eternal life?" he asked. Maybe he thought Jesus would stumble around for an answer or say something offensive to the Jewish law.

Instead, Jesus used the most effective method in teaching. He returned the question by asking the lawyer what he understood the Law to say on the subject.

In response, the lawyer quoted from Deuteronomy 6:5 and Leviticus 19:18:

> Thou shalt love the Lord thy God with all thy heart, and with all thy soul, and with all thy strength, and with all thy mind; and thy neighbor as thyself (Luke 10:27).

When Jesus agreed with him that this was the way to inherit eternal life, the lawyer persisted with what he thought was a real stickler of a question. "And who is my neighbor?" he asked, probably with a trace of sarcasm in his voice (v. 29).

Jesus was not to be trapped into a philosophical discussion. Instead, He told a story. Before it was over, the lawyer's question had to be rephrased. After describing the actions of the three men who came upon the injured man lying by the roadside, Jesus asked the lawyer who he thought had acted like a neighbor.

The lawyer answered, "He that showed mercy on him" (v. 37). Jesus told him to follow this example in his quest for eternal life.

To Whom Am I a Neighbor?

Now the question was—and remains for us to answer for ourselves—not who is my neighbor, but to whom should I be a neighbor? The definition of "neighbor" in Jesus' teaching is the person who shows mercy to another.

I think we will all readily admit there are people all around us who need to be shown mercy. The battered and bruised souls of this world are living in our own neighborhoods. The tragedy is that too often we don't know how much the people next door need an act of mercy from us till it is too late.

We hear through the neighborhood "grapevine" that John and Sue are divorced. "That nice young couple!" we exclaim in surprise. We thought they had everything going for them.

We shake our heads over the delinquency of the teenager down the street, and we are utterly shocked when we hear about a suicide in the community. These people need to experience God's mercy through us—the care and witness of a Christian neighbor.

The question of our relationship with our neighbors was very important to Jesus. Another man also came to Jesus one day and asked how to obtain eternal life. Matthew 19:16-22 tells the story. Jesus told him to keep the commandments and specifically included, "Thou shalt love thy neighbor as thyself."

When put to the test of proving his love by selling his possessions and giving to the poor, the young man drew back. He couldn't part with his material goods, not even to help those who had nothing.

We who know the Lord have so much. We are rich in Him. The apostle Paul tells us in Ephesians 1:3 that we are blessed "with all spiritual blessings in heavenly places in Christ." Our sins are forgiven. He has made available to us His wisdom. We have obtained an eternal inheritance, we have received the Holy Spirit, and we know what it is to be loved by the Heavenly Father. These are but a few of the blessings Paul talks about.

Paul also reminds us in Ephesians 2 that at one time we were "dead in trespasses and sins." We also "walked according to the course of this world . . . and were by nature the children of wrath" (vv. 1-3). Our non-Christian neighbors now labor under this burden from which we are freed.

For example, when a wife displeases her non-Christian husband, it is not likely he will respond in a spirit of mercy because he is dead to godly attributes. Being a child of wrath, the only response he knows is to retaliate in some way. Some non-Christians react more violently than others in similar situations. Some react with physical violence, others use verbal violence. Both are damaging to relationships and we find the results in the suffering, battered wives and mothers in our neighborhoods.

You don't have to sit over a cup of coffee with your neighbors very long before you'll hear tales of abuse and mistrust. The yards may be well-groomed and the houses freshly painted, but that is no indication of what is going on behind the closed doors and drawn drapes.

I'm not trying to take you into an imaginary world,

nor am I a pessimist. We must be realistic and look beyond the surface—behind the facade most people display to the world. What is behind the rising divorce rates? Do people just politely, with "please" and "thank you" thrown in, ask for and give those divorces to each other? Of course not. There is apathy, anger, disappointment, lying, and cheating—and sometimes physical violence.

All this is going on in the real world of our neighborhoods. The important question is how are we viewing these neighbors in need?

Jesus' Compassion

Matthew 9:36 tells us how Jesus viewed the people He saw:

> But when he saw the multitudes he was moved with compassion on them, because they fainted, and were scattered abroad, as sheep having no shepherd.

When we look at our neighbors we usually see that Betty is always working in her yard. She certainly loves gardening, we think. And we get nervous when our dog runs through her flowerbeds. Or we wish Mary would make her rowdy boys stay home. Or we get a little envious when we see Shirley in another new outfit.

Maybe we enjoy having coffee with the neighbors or doing crafts together. Exchanging baby-sitting and recipes can be convenient and helpful. We may even wish the family across the street would bring their children to Sunday school, as we rush off to another church meeting.

All these reactions to our neighbors are natural. But do we ever look on them with compassion? Do we realize they have spiritual needs only the Lord can meet? He looks on our neighbors with compassion.

Karen had lived in her neighborhood for several years. One night she woke out of a sound sleep with the thought going through her mind, "What am I doing for the Lord? What about my neighbors?" She was deeply impressed that God was speaking to her.

Karen enjoyed entertaining. She came to me and said, "I want to have a Bible study in my home but I need someone to lead it." We both felt God had the right person to minister to her neighbors. After praying for God's wisdom, Suzanne came to mind.

Suzanne was a new Christian and had been a member of the group I was leading. When she met that first day with Karen's neighbors we knew God had led us in our choice. Sitting in Karen's living room were several women who had known Suzanne in her preconversion days. In the weeks that followed those women saw with their own eyes and heard with their own ears the change in Suzanne. Jesus had become a living reality in her life.

Spiritual Hunger

The Scripture says that Jesus viewed the people as sheep without a shepherd. The purpose of a shepherd is to care for the sheep and lead them to food.

People today are not only experiencing deep hurts due to circumstances in their lives, they are also suffering from spiritual starvation. Possibly because of physical and social needs, we see a growing hunger for spiritual reality.

One evening Sonja's husband told her that a business associate had asked if she would contact his wife. "Marlyce needs help," he said.

The next day Sonja dropped in at the Christian bookstore. Marlyce was there, wandering among the bookshelves. When Sonja greeted her, Marlyce mentioned she often came there because she found such a feeling of peace in the store. Sonja invited her to her Bible study, and Marlyce accepted without hesitation.

One Tuesday morning Sonja felt impressed that Marlyce was ready to accept the Lord. But when Sonja asked her if she would, Marlyce declined.

The following night Marlyce awakened. As if a voice were speaking in the dark, the words came to her, "Are you ready to serve Me?" She asked where she was supposed to go. The thought came, "Pastor Cole's." The next morning she hurried to the parsonage, and Jean Cole, the pastor's wife, led her to an experience of real peace in Jesus Christ.

That was Thursday, the day Marlyce had planned to go to the doctor for more tranquilizers. Instead she called and told him she would no longer need the pills; she now had Jesus in her life.

Sonja became a true neighbor to Marlyce when she invited her to the Bible study. Marlyce's need was such that only God could meet it. Underneath her hurts and her need for tranquilizers was a spiritual hunger. The women in our neighborhoods who are hurting don't always realize the answer to their problems is Jesus Christ. They don't know that at the bottom of their searching is a spiritual hunger.

"Felt" Need vs. "Real" Need

Jesus made a comparison between "felt" need and "real" need when talking to a multitude of people who had followed Him to the other side of the Sea of Galilee. The day before He had miraculously multiplied five loaves of bread and two fish to meet their "felt" need.

Like most of us, their sense of physical preservation was acute. And when they found someone who could so easily—it seemed to them—silence their hunger pangs they naturally followed Him.

Jesus used it as an opportunity to teach an eternal truth. He first made them realize He knew their motives: "Ye seek me, not because ye saw the miracles, but because ye did eat of the loaves, and were filled" (John 6:26).

People don't always come to hear what the Bible says or to learn about Jesus out of pure motives. Their search is not always obviously spiritual. But if we want to follow Jesus' pattern, we don't have the right to turn them away. Instead, their "felt" needs or interests can sometimes be turned into a bridge between the material and the spiritual.

This is what Jesus did in the next verse. He used something they understood to give them a spiritual truth: "Labor not for the meat which perisheth, but for that meat which endureth unto everlasting life, which the Son of man shall give unto you" (John 6:27).

Jesus was not promoting welfare cases. He never condoned laziness. He was speaking of priorities.

Spiritual Priorities

We in America have followed a set of priorities determined by a materialistic society for a number of years now. While much of the world goes to bed hungry, we are so well fed we don't even wake up wanting breakfast. Our insatiable desire for affluence led to the alienation of our youth during the 1960's. They turned their backs on the "Establishment" and in their anguish they marched, rioted, and yelled their protests in four-letter words. But their spiritual hunger persisted.

It is quieter now in the 1970's. The hippies don't line the streets in the university district like they once did. You can walk on the campus without fear of being barricaded in a building. The police aren't marching double file along the paths anymore. But the spiritual hunger is still there. In fact, it is more evident now.

Our youth are turning to Yoga, Zen, and meditation. In their quest for peace they have slumped at the feet of the eastern gurus. Not all our youth, of course, but a significant number. There is reason to be concerned.

These young people are spiritually hungry because they haven't been given the "meat which endureth unto everlasting life." Who should have given it to them? The older generation—their parents, our peers. But as we look at their parents we realize they don't have this "meat" to give. They too are trying to satisfy their own hunger—in their own way. They pursue pleasure, the acquisition of possessions, and bow at the feet of intellectual enlightenment.

Ignorance is not bliss. If we read the signs correctly we must realize the constant searching and aberrant behavior patterns in our society today are symptoms of deep spiritual hunger in the hearts of people.

Jesus' message for these spiritually hungry neighbors is the same today as it was for those who followed Him to the other side of the Sea of Galilee: "Labor not for the meat which perisheth, but for that meat which endureth unto everlasting life" (John 6:27).

Our Bible-study group had been meeting for a couple of years when someone invited Helen. She entered into our discussions with enthusiasm, but frankly admitted she was also interested in Zen and Yoga.

"I take the good from Zen and Yoga and put it with what I learn here," she told us one day. "That way I get what I want."

Like so many people today, Helen had turned to spiritual substitutes to satisfy that unexplainable hunger. But Jesus said: "I am the bread of life: he that cometh to me shall never hunger; and he that believeth on me shall never thirst" (John 6:35).

When Mary Larrimore arrived for her first day of meeting with a small group of women for Bible study in Taunton, Massachusetts, she found such spiritual hunger among them she was overwhelmed. Together, week by week, they discussed and explored the Scriptures.

"Their spiritual desire," she says, "reminded me of a dry and thirsty land where no water is, and Christ's words, 'They that hunger and thirst after righteousness shall be filled,' became my desire for them."

As these women found the answers to their questions in the Word of God, they began to invite their friends, neighbors, and relatives, and the group enlarged. As Jesus proved himself to be the Bread of Life to them, about 20 women were touched for Jesus Christ within a little over a year.

From observation, we realize we have a twofold situation today that can be made to work in favor of neighborhood evangelism. Subject to their own sinful nature, people are truly neighbors in need. At the same time, we are living in a time of spiritual hunger the world has not seen for many years.

Encounter With God

That first Friday afternoon all 14 women listened with intense interest as Inga, our guest speaker, told of her life during World War II. She had experienced God's keeping power when in danger from enemy soldiers. She told how she, a young teenager, along with her family escaped from Poland to East Germany and finally to West Germany, with the Russian soldiers in pursuit.

At the close of the meeting Anna came up to me and said in a strong German accent, "Someday I want to tell you my story."

I smiled, remarked that I would like to hear it, and went on to other things. Little did we realize God had that afternoon brought together two women from the same part of the world, with similar experiences. For one, at least, it was a crossroads in her life. But we had prayed that God would bring to the study the women He wanted there.

Anna continued to come week after week. She read the Scripture verses we asked her to but, other than that, she sat silently through the discussion and prayer time. But the seeds of God's Word were taking root in her heart.

Six months after we had started, we invited the

women to attend a musicale at Calvary Temple, Seattle. Several came, including Anna. At the close of the service, one of our Christian members talked to Anna about surrendering her life to Jesus Christ. While sitting in her seat she quiétly responded and God did something in her heart at that moment.

Later that same evening over coffee, Anna told us how she had been living in Berlin during World War II and had narrowly escaped being killed in several bombings. After coming to the United States she married and eventually moved to the neighborhood where we were now having a Bible study.

One day a year or two before the study had begun, Anna and her husband Frank were driving along the freeway past Calvary Temple in Seattle. Anna turned to Frank and said, "Someday I want you to take me to that church."

Frank had never taken her. He wasn't particularly interested in church. But God granted her desire through the Bible-study group. Anna went home from the musicale that Sunday evening and began to read the Bible, both to herself and aloud to Frank.

A year passed and Frank grew very weak from heart trouble. The women planned a potluck supper for their husbands, to be held at the home next door to Anna's. Anna begged Frank to come. He was barely able to make it up the steps into the house. But he stayed through the supper and for a film on the Holy Land.

In the early hours of the next morning, Frank passed out of this life into the next. We don't know if he had made peace with the Lord, but we do know that because of the neighborhood Bible study he'd heard the gospel message before he died—not only through Anna, but through the narration with the film.

The women in the Bible-study group cooked dinner for the family the day of the funeral. Some of Anna's and Frank's friends remarked, "We wish we had friends like this."

Beyond the Society of Saints

God is totally involved in neighborhood evangelism. As in the experience of Anna and Frank, the Lord is calling people to come to himself. He is a God of love, and He expresses it in His attitude toward men and women while they are still dead in their sins. Second Peter 3:9 says: "The Lord is . . . not willing that any should perish, but that all should come to repentance."

And in Ezekiel 33:11 He says: "As I live, saith the Lord God, I have no pleasure in the death of the wicked; but that the wicked turn from his way and live."

He not only takes no pleasure in the death of the wicked—God is not cruel and He doesn't want anyone to perish—He also doesn't try to get even. Instead, God has taken positive action in loving the world. His love embraced the idea and worked out the details for our salvation. His love sacrificed His only Son for our redemption. And His love extends beyond our little society of saints to those neighbors who do not know Him.

But God does not come along and hit people with a thunderbolt of love. He doesn't just put a good feeling into their hearts and then cause them to look up and say, "Ah, now I know God loves me." It doesn't work that way.

How does it work? Paul, in 2 Corinthians 5:14, says the love of Christ constrained or, more literally, controlled him. He makes this statement in the middle of a paragraph describing his relationship with both the Corinthian Christians and also with the world outside the church.

To understand Paul's line of thought in this paragraph will help us understand God's plan for showing His love to our non-Christian neighbors. He is saying it is Christ's love for him that controls his actions toward others, Christian and non-Christian alike. This love was demonstrated to all men by Christ's death for all, resulting in our reconciliation to God our Father. And this love now works through us to bring others into this same experience.

We are to be ministers of reconciliation. To say it another way, we are to be channels through which God's love can flow into the lives of those around us.

During His life on earth, Jesus' whole thrust was to reconcile people to His Heavenly Father. In doing so, He left both teaching and example for us to follow.

Value of One Person

Jesus' teaching explored the concept of God's love for the whole world and laid out the plan for reaching those who need to be reached.

Both Matthew and Luke record the Parable of the Lost Sheep. Luke tells us that as Jesus was speaking to the publicans and sinners, the Pharisees and scribes made a snide remark: "This man receiveth sinners, and eateth with them" (Luke 15:2).

In response to their critical attitude, Jesus told how a shepherd would leave a flock of 99 sheep and go out to find and rescue one lost sheep. Jesus went on to describe the joyous return of the shepherd, not just leading the sheep but carrying it on his shoulders and entreating his friends to rejoice with him over the found sheep. Why rejoice? The natural response to finding any lost object, a sheep, a coin, or a prodigal is elation.

"But to go after only one when you already have 99 secure in your possession? Can't you be satisfied with what you have?" someone may ask. Jesus' answer penetrated the hearts of His self-appointed critics. He contrasted their disdain of publicans and sinners with the reaction in heaven over finding one lost sheep: "Likewise joy shall be in heaven over one sinner that repenteth, more than over ninety and nine just persons, which need no repentance" (Luke 15:7).

Those scribes and Pharisees may not have understood the full meaning of this Parable of the Lost Sheep. But I am sure most of us do. It fully displays God's value system in relation to the non-Christian—that person who lives next door and does not know Jesus Christ as Saviour.

Jesus explained this value system more explicitly when He said: "For what shall it profit a man, if he shall gain the whole world, and lose his own soul? Or what shall a man give in exchange for his soul?" (Mark 8:36, 37).

There is nothing in this world of more value than an eternal soul. It is as simple as that. That was the reason Jesus came to live among men. It was the reason for His life-style, His teaching, and His works. And it was the reason for His death—even the way He died—and His resurrection. So that "whosoever will" might have eternal life in Him.

What is the reason for our living? Does our life-style tell the world what value we place on an eternal soul? When our spirits are touched by the Holy Spirit are we free of guilt about our relationships with our neighbors?

The apostle John says, "He that saith he abideth in

27

him ought himself also so to walk, even as he walked" (1 John 2:6).

How do we feel about our words and our deeds before the dying world?

Bridge Builders

Jesus' works were consistent with His words. They complemented each other. We have an example in the story of Jesus' healing the man sick of the palsy in Mark 2:1-12. He told the skeptical scribes—the armchair critics of the day—that the healing of the sick man was an outward demonstration of His power to forgive sins.

In the story of the feeding of the 5,000, we see a progression in the example Jesus gave us. He was first moved by compassion to teach the multitude. This same compassion compelled Him also to take care of their physical needs, which in turn served as a bridge for more teaching the next day about the Bread of Life.

If we walk as Jesus walked, we will become bridge builders for Him. The events of our lives will take on a spiritual significance that we will be able to share with others. This does not call for a superspiritual attitude or a mystical interpretation of life. It is simply committing all things to Him and recognizing His power at work in our lives.

I had been leading the neighborhood Bible study for about a year when my mother became seriously ill. She was hospitalized and it was my responsibility to provide her with the supportive relationship she needed at that time. For 5 weeks I drove 60 miles round trip every day to see her. During that period our son who was in college in St. Louis was also hospitalized.

Torn between the needs of my mother and my son, I was almost beside myself. I didn't know whether to set up housekeeping at my mother's bedside or to catch the next plane for St. Louis.

A well-meaning individual advised me to give up the Bible study. My first responsibility was to my mother, she said.

But I did not feel free to leave the Bible study. Instead I shared my burden with the group and they responded in love and prayers. Those women began to support me. But it also became a learning experience for them. As they learned of the power of God to sustain in the midst of life's trials, their faith grew along with mine.

Jesus, the Example

Jesus did much of His bridge building in homes around the dinner table. In Matthew 9:10-13 we find Him eating a meal with publicans and sinners. When the Pharisees saw this, they crowded around Jesus' disciples and scornfully asked, "Why eateth your master with publicans and sinners?"

Jesus overheard this. Before the frustrated disciples could answer, He replied with a sharpness that must have pierced the Pharisees to the marrow. He said: "They that be whole need not a physician, but they that are sick . . . . I am not come to call the righteous, but sinners to repentance" (vv. 12, 13).

And that is why He, who was God in the flesh, was eating with sinners. He was showing us how to build bridges.

He also built a bridge to walk across into Zaccheus' life. Zaccheus was a curious little man. He had, no doubt, heard many stories of spectacular events surrounding Jesus, so he swallowed his pride and climbed a tree to peer over the heads of the crowd.

But just looking at Jesus would have done little for Zaccheus. Jesus knew He needed to establish a relationship with him, so He called Zaccheus to come down. Jesus even invited himself to be a guest in Zaccheus' home. The Scriptures relate that Zaccheus "made haste, and came down, and received him joyfully" (Luke 19:6).

In the past I have purposely visited in neighbors' homes, determined to build bridges. Without exception I have felt a warm gratitude on the part of my hostess for the short time spent together.

But let me say quickly that both the wisdom and the gentleness of the Holy Spirit must guide the Christian in visiting neighbors. It would accomplish no good at all to intrude unwanted. If you are unsure of a welcome, it would be best to invite that neighbor to your home first.

Abundant Opportunities

If we are alert, we can often find beautiful reasons to make a visit and begin establishing a relationship. Why not call on the young couple with a new baby? They couldn't resent your bringing a small gift. Or how about a plate of cookies for the family moving in down the street? Do you raise flowers or vegetables? Have you ever shared them with that neighbor with whom you have only a "waving" acquaintance?

A coffee klatch in your home will open many neighbors' doors. Proverbs 18:24 tells us, "A man that hath friends must show himself friendly."

One day I was having tea with a neighbor when she began to relate her fears about raising her two small sons in today's troubled world. I agreed with her that it is a frightening task, and I shared how

God's Word had guided me in raising my own children. This conversation provided an opportunity to invite her to a home Bible study, and she quickly accepted.

She came to the study and was soon one of our most enthusiastic members. It wasn't long until she brought another neighbor.

Sometime later she said to me, "Do you remember when I first started coming that I left myself a way out? I made all kinds of excuses, like, 'I'll try it,' and, 'If the boys get along with the baby-sitter,' and so on." But she went on to say that because of our friendship she had kept coming, and now she would not miss the weekly study for anything.

Because of our friendship she was opening her heart and mind to God's Word every week, something she had not done in many years. And I began to understand what it takes to build a bridge for the Lord.

Our neighbors are looking for friendship from us. The dictionary defines *reconcile* as a restoring of friendship, harmony, or communion. Before most people can be restored to communion with God, they need our friendship. This is God's plan for evangelization. When we encounter God in our own lives this is what He asks of us: to be ministers of reconciliation to a neighbor in need by first being a friend. Are we willing?

Alive and Active

Raised in a Christian home, Donna drifted away from the Lord and the church during her college years. "I had accepted Jesus as Saviour when a child," she recalls, "but during those late teens my faith was never seriously challenged. As a result my spiritual life did not continue to develop."

About a month after our Bible study began, someone invited Donna to attend. We were studying the Gospel of Mark. "As I began attending," she says, "suddenly I was hearing reinforcements of what I had learned as a child in Sunday school and church."

"It was exciting," she continues, "to hear other people discuss the Bible, then look into it myself and pull it all together. I had heard these things in sermons many times, I'm sure. But the truths of God's Word became real during that period of my life."

Donna sprang alive spiritually during the next couple of years as we studied first Mark, then the prophecies of Jesus' second coming, John, Acts, and Romans. The Bible study filled a need in her life and the desire to share what she learned grew until she couldn't contain it.

Donna became deeply concerned about the spiritual

needs of her six children. Two of them were already in college, but her vital witness soon became an influence for righteousness in their lives.

Then Donna felt impressed to do something about giving the gospel to the children of the neighborhood. In the spring she started with 10 to 12 children meeting every week in her living room. By fall she had two groups. From 25 to 30 children heard the good news every week and many accepted Jesus into their hearts.

In a year and a half over 100 children listened to the gospel in these children's groups. And it all began when the seed of God's Word burst forth in life-giving faith in Donna's heart.

God's Word is alive and active. We had determined from the first day of our Bible study to accept the Word as our final authority in all discussions. We also put our faith in the Word as the dynamic that would bring about change in these women's lives. We were not disappointed. The chain of events in Donna's life was but one example.

God's Purpose

During the early days of our neighborhood Bible study, Isaiah 55:10, 11 became very real to me. I memorized these verses and quoted them often to myself and to others:

> For as the rain cometh down, and the snow from heaven, and returneth not thither, but watereth the earth, and maketh it bring forth and bud, that it may give seed to the sower, and bread to the eater: so shall my word be that goeth forth out of my mouth: it shall not return unto me void, but it shall accomplish that which I please, and it shall prosper in the thing whereto I sent it.

The promise of God is that His Word will not return void, it will accomplish God's purpose. Sometimes we may not see the immediate accomplishment of that purpose. It may take months or even years for the seeds of God's Word to bear fruit in the lives of those we minister to.

I find I need to remind myself occasionally of the farming process. Planting, cultivating, and watering precede harvesting. From the apostle Paul we learn that some plant and some water, but God gives the increase. If we are faithful sowers of the seed, dependable cultivators and waterers, often God allows us the joy of participating in the harvest.

Yet there are those who do not accept the Lord immediately. Should we feel our efforts are in vain? No, for Paul tells us in Romans 10:14:

> How then shall they call on him in whom they have not believed? and how shall they believe in him of whom they have not heard? and how shall they hear without a preacher?

They have to hear the gospel before they can believe. The seed has to be planted before the crop can be harvested. And the time between planting and harvesting varies with the type of crop.

An interesting story came out of Akita, Japan a few years ago. It was reported that several seeds had been found in an ancient tomb. Archaeologists believed them to be 4,000 years old. The amazing discovery was that when they were exposed to sunlight those ancient seeds sprouted!

The seed of God's Word never loses its germination power. As in Donna's experience, the Word can lie dormant for years. Then God can bring a person into a situation where the seed will burst and bring forth fruit. God truly gives the increase.

Salvation Through the Word

In a neighborhood Bible study Paul's statement in 2 Timothy 3:15 becomes a contemporary reality: "The holy Scriptures... are able to make thee wise unto salvation through faith which is in Christ Jesus."

The plan of salvation is in the Scripture, waiting to be discovered by the open, inquiring mind. It is so evident that sometimes even the closed mind cannot escape the truth. A dramatic example is given by D. James Kennedy in his book *Spiritual Renewal.*

Kennedy tells about Frank Morrison who half a century ago determined to prove that the story of the resurrection of Jesus Christ was nothing but a good story. Morrison, a young lawyer, turned his trained mind to a search for what he thought was the truth. He gathered the information, studied the testimonies to the Resurrection, and weighed seriously everything he found connected with the evidence.

At the conclusion of his exhaustive investigation, Morrison wrote his book *Who Moved the Stone?* It was not the attack on the Resurrection he had originally planned, but one of the most important books ever written proving the truth of the resurrection of Jesus Christ.

The Scriptures had made Frank Morrison "wise unto salvation." Serious study can do the same for our neighbors. As women open up their minds to the teaching of the Word, their thinking about spiritual things changes and their lives take on a new style of living when they accept Jesus as Saviour.

Judy was one of those for whom the Bible study brought a change in her life. She says:

> After I made a mess of things and of my marriage, I found I do need guidelines even though I am an adult. I still need to learn moral right and wrong. It's too easy to become wrapped up in yourself and your

own personal desires whether they hurt someone else or not.

The home Bible studies helped me in my family life. I learned that Jesus taught that there are solutions to our problems. He even taught me how to be happily married. But to hear the Word of God we must have sources. For me it is the home Bible study in our area. We can take our personal everyday problems and learn how Jesus would have us solve them. This has meant a great deal to me in the last year since I started the Bible study. And it has changed my life into a very satisfying life.

Although written more than 2,000 years ago in a prescientific age, the Bible is up-to-date in its answers to people's problems. More than one marriage has been helped through a neighborhood Bible study. Not because it is a book of rules. It is not. But God speaks to us through the lives, thoughts, experiences, struggles, successes, and failures of men and women who lived in a real world. As we share in their joys and sorrows, we can identify with them and follow their examples. We can learn by observing how God dealt with them and how they responded to God.

As we discuss their lives and the life-changing truths that emerge from their experiences, the women in our groups sense the relevancy of God's Word and their faith in the eternal merciful God grows. Paul says in Romans 10:17: "So then faith cometh by hearing, and hearing by the word of God."

Worth Studying

It is important how the Bible is studied in our groups. A survey was taken of 300,000 people in neighborhood Bible studies. It was found that about 70 percent of these had never studied the Bible before.

In ministering to women who have not opened a Bible since Sunday school days, or maybe never, we must believe the Bible is worth studying. Before you judge that statement as being simplistic, think about where most of us go for spiritual and emotional support in times of distress. Is it to God's Word? Or do we run to a friend for counsel? Or read a book by a well-known author?

We tend to be experience-oriented. Most of us like a good story and are drawn to a listening ear. We probably spend more time reading popular Christian books than we do the Word of God. From these books we learn our doctrine, gain inspiration, and determine what Christians should act like.

But 2 Timothy 3:16, 17 says that Scripture is for our understanding of doctrine, for reproving us when we do wrong, and for our instruction in how to do right. This follows the experience of salvation which also is made known to us through the study of the Word.

To believe the Bible is worth studying means putting it first in our own lives. Books by our fellow Christians are worthwhile—I wouldn't be writing one if I didn't believe that—but they can never take the place of our own personal involvement with the Word of God.

Next we must believe that people are brought to a commitment to Jesus not by our words or experiences, as inspirational as they may be, but by the power of conviction in the Word. First Peter 1:23 says: "Being born again, not of corruptible seed, but of incorruptible, by the word of God, which liveth and abideth forever."

This does not mean we should never share our ideas and experiences. These do have a place in the application of God's Word to our lives. But we must first start by reading the Scripture and discovering what it says and means.

In our neighborhood Bible study we never knew from one week to the next what comments to expect from some of the women. But we found that there was little argument when we stayed in the Word. When we began to quote men's sayings or introduce our own opinions we ran into dissension.

Inductive Bible Study

People often try to rewrite the Bible to fit their own ideas. Our responsibility as leaders is to help the group observe what it really says. This is done best by the inductive method of Bible study.

Inductive Bible study consists of three steps: observation, interpretation, and application. Each of these steps is of equal importance. To leave one out is to leave the group with an inadequate view of the Scripture.

Observation simply means asking, "What does it say?" Look at the people in the passage being studied; how they are described and the relationships they have with each other. When studying the Gospels, notice especially each person's relationship with Jesus Christ. The place of action, the time, the events, the commands given, and the promises made are all important.

In interpretation we ask, "What does it mean?" Sometimes we need help understanding the different customs. Definitions should be looked up in dictionaries and Bible dictionaries. Sometimes the cultural background should be researched. A Bible handbook is helpful, as are maps. Relationships should be explored and interpreted.

The last step in inductive Bible study is sometimes neglected, yet no study is complete without it. Application is asking, "What does it mean to me?" For the Word of God to become effective in our lives, we have to apply the main points of the study to our own lives. The Word must make a difference in our attitude and obedience toward God, in our attitude toward ourselves, and in the situations and relationships in our families.

Throughout the Bible study we should not refer to commentaries for help. The purpose of the Bible study is to lead our neighbors into discovering for *themselves* what God's Word says. Even in our own preparation it is best to leave the commentaries untouched. We want to get the Word into our own hearts as we prepare.

Study guides, such as the one at the end of this book, are helpful to the leader. You will notice it consists only of questions. There is very little comment accompanying any of the lessons. The questions in this study guide and the others recommended in the resource material section are structured to lead the group into an inductive Bible study. The questions were formulated to cover all three steps.

Adequate personal preparation by the leader consists of the following:

1. Read the chapter as many times as necessary for clear understanding.

2. Do your own thinking, using the three steps in inductive Bible study.

3. Review the questions in the study guide.

Some General Rules

Just as certain ingredients are necessary to bake a good cake, so there are certain things that produce a successful Bible study. Our objective behind these rules is to bring our non-Christian neighbors into a relationship with Jesus Christ.

The first rule is to introduce the group to Jesus Christ. We don't conduct Bible studies to preach our church doctrines or promote church membership, although both of these may eventually be dealt with—after that neighbor becomes reconciled to the Lord. Our reason for existing as a small group in our neighborhood is evangelistic—to introduce neighbors who will not come to our churches to Jesus Christ.

Second, the Bible is our authority in our discussions. Most non-Christians won't accept the Bible as the inspired Word of God, and we shouldn't try to force it on them. We have to believe the Bible will speak for itself—and it will! But we can lay a ground rule for our study sessions. We can say, "For our discussion the document is our authority. We want to find out what it has to say to 20th-century women." Our neighbors will accept that kind of reasoning.

Third, the Bible should be studied by Books or units. It was given in book form so it is logical to the non-Christian to study it that way.

We are there to minister to their needs and a little consideration of their feelings will go a long way toward building a bridge for Jesus to walk across into their lives. Everyone, Christian and non-Christian alike, needs equal opportunity to be involved in the excitement of discovering what is in the Bible. The study, therefore, needs to be structured so no background knowledge is required. This is not very difficult. It only requires sticking to the passage being studied. It is permissible to refer to verses already studied but not to go ahead or jump around the Bible trying to find proof texts. By staying on the passage being studied, week by week a framework is built, within which the claims of Jesus Christ will be considered.

In any group there are times when someone will be

tempted to go off on a tangent. This should be avoided at all costs! Often it ends up in an argument which detracts from the study. If someone has an honest question that is not related to the study, it can be handled later with that person alone.

Another courtesy we owe our neighbors in the study of God's Word is the use of a modern translation. Most non-Christians today are unfamiliar with not only the Bible but also with King James English. When I start a new group, I buy enough copies of *Good News for Modern Man* to go around. It is inexpensive and written in contemporary language—language that everyone can understand.

By doing this, another problem is solved. Instead of asking the group to turn to Luke 4 for the first study, I can ask them to turn to a certain page. Again, they are familiar with this method in the use of books and it saves embarrassment for those who may not know where Luke is in the Bible.

It has been exciting to watch the women after a few weeks of Bible study show up with new Bibles they have found in their own ventures into Christian bookstores. Many never entered these stores before and they come to the group excited about their new find.

The Word of God is alive and active and it will not return void when we carefully sow the seed in the hearts of our neighbors.

5

Enabling of the Spirit

For several years, Phyllis watched young couples move into her neighborhood, establish their homes, and begin to raise families. A burden for their eternal welfare grew in her heart, prompting her to reach out to them by inviting the wives to visit with her over a cup of coffee.

But Phyllis was a little older than these women, her family almost raised, and the neighbors knew she was a Christian. They always seemed to stand just beyond her reach.

Then one Sunday she discovered a new dimension in witnessing. A new family visited the Assembly of God she attends and told of winning neighbors to Jesus Christ through conducting Bible studies in their home.

Immediately Phyllis felt this was something she would like to do. She began to make plans and to read material on the subject. She felt she needed to establish the Bible as God's Word, so she visited a Christian bookstore and chose a course dealing with the authority of the Word.

Daily she intended to call her neighbors, but something always came up that caused her to put it off until the next day. This went on for 6 months.

Finally the day after New Year's, God spoke to her while she was scrubbing her kitchen floor. She knew she was to call her neighbors that day. It was so clear and forceful she immediately stopped scrubbing and put the mop down.

Then she began to argue with the quiet but firm voice within. She made the usual excuses, but the impression that today was the day persisted. By nightfall she had called all 14 of her neighbors. She told them she had been thinking about the mess the world is in and that maybe the Bible had some answers for all of us. Then she invited them to come to her house to talk about it.

When the appointed day came, 12 out of the 14 walked into Phyllis' living room carrying their Bibles under their arms. One of the women later told Phyllis that the day before Christmas, while a couple of the neighbors had been together making candles, they had discussed the need for such a Bible study. This was a confirmation to Phyllis that God had truly spoken to her and it was His time for the neighborhood to come together to study His Word.

At the very first meeting one of the women said, "We've read the Bible, and we can't understand it."

Phyllis laid out a number of modern translations. She had them read both Psalm 23 and the Beatitudes from each translation so the women could compare them. Most of them said they hadn't realized various translations were available, and they became excited about the Bible itself.

Then Phyllis suggested they let her obtain a copy of *Good News for Modern Man* for each of them. She explained it would be helpful in their study if they all had the same modern translation and this particular one was available in an inexpensive edition.

Need for the Spirit's Guidance

As the weeks went by, the Bible course she had chosen for the group to study became a jumping-off point. The women came with questions about what they had been reading in the Word during the week at home.

"Say, before we begin, could you explain this to me?" started discussions from time to time on the Holy Spirit, divine healing, and the Second Coming. Over and over different ones in the group commented, "Why hasn't my church taught me this?"

Because of their hunger for learning what the Bible teaches and the unpredictability of the questions, Phyllis found it impossible to prepare ahead in the usual way. Instead she quietly sat before the Lord in prayer prior to each meeting, meditating and praying for the group and for His wisdom in answering their inquiries.

Each week as she thought back over the answers that had come to her mind during the meeting, she never regretted anything. She never wished she had said either more or less. The Lord truly had spoken through His Word to meet the needs of each woman who came searching.

After the group had been meeting for a number of weeks, Phyllis introduced the idea of praying. The women decided to write a summary of their hour's discussion and offer that as a prayer. After more consideration they finally said, "Phyllis, the truth is we don't know how to pray. Will you teach us?" She shared with them how she had prayed in different circumstances—when faced with discouragements, trials, sickness—and how God had answered.

A few days later one of the women came rushing over to Phyllis' house. She had been afflicted with a fungus for months and the doctor had been unable to find any medicine that would remove it. After the previous meeting and their discussion on prayer, she had prayed about it and God had healed her.

The next meeting was charged with new excitement generated by their experiences in prayer. One woman had always gone into her closet to pray, but during the past week she prayed wherever she was as she went about her daily tasks. She also began to pray with her children.

When summer came and school was out, it became difficult for the mothers to continue the weekly Bible study. They decided to disband until school started again in the fall.

When the weekly Bible study resumed, 10 women returned. That year they began to seek the Baptism. Two received the infilling of the Spirit in the privacy of their homes, another at an area-wide charismatic meeting.

At the end of 2 years Phyllis felt her ministry to the group was over. God sent another woman to lead it and it continued to meet for another year.

As Phyllis says, "Groups need to die." The women needed to enter into the life and fellowship of the church. They became involved—some in churches they had grown up in, others in Assembly of God congregations.

The story of Phyllis' Bible study is unique. It did not follow the exact pattern we talked about in the last chapter like most groups do. But the characteristic her ministry had in common with all who witness to their neighbors was her reliance on the guidance of the Spirit.

The Holy Spirit in Evangelism

Let's see how the Holy Spirit, the Third Person of the Trinity, is involved in neighborhood evangelism.

As in Phyllis' experience, the Holy Spirit will take charge of who attends our Bible studies if we allow Him. And He will work in their individual lives. Without the Holy Spirit's involvement in our ministry to non-Christians, we are helpless. Paul says in 1 Corinthians 2:14: "But the natural man receiveth not the things of the Spirit of God: for they are foolishness unto him: neither can he know them, because they are spiritually discerned."

And in 2 Corinthians 4:3, 4 he says:

> But if our gospel be hid, it is hid to them that are lost: in whom the god of this world hath blinded the minds of them which believe not, lest the light of the glorious gospel of Christ, who is the image of God, should shine unto them.

Because of the distortion of human minds by sin it is impossible to persuade them of righteousness through human reason alone. The Word of God, breathed into by the Holy Spirit, and the anointing of the Spirit on our words are needed to penetrate their darkened hearts.

How did you and I come to believe in Jesus as our personal Saviour? "For God, who commanded the light to shine out of darkness, hath shined in our hearts, to give the light of the knowledge of the glory of God in the face of Jesus Christ" (2 Corinthians 4:6).

The revelation of the truth of God's message has to come from God himself. The Spirit of God must connect with the spirit of man, confirming within that this is right. It is not just an intellectual piece of knowledge that can be passed on like facts and figures. Although the mind is involved, the content of the gospel is spiritually discerned.

Jesus gives us some insight into the operation of the Holy Spirit in the non-Christian's life. In John

16:8-11, He says the Holy Spirit will reprove or, more literally, convince of sin, righteousness, and judgment. In this convincing process the Holy Spirit brings about the conversion of the non-Christian.

Power to Witness

Somehow in all this God wants to involve us. It's not that He couldn't bring people to himself without our help. But He has given us the privilege of being partners with Him in the ministry of reconciliation. Our part is to be witnesses. And we who are Pentecostal have a great responsibility. When Jesus was talking intimately with His disciples just before His ascension, He said: "But ye shall receive power, after that the Holy Ghost is come upon you: and ye shall be witnesses unto me . . ." (Acts 1:8).

This verse and Acts 2:4 are probably the most quoted Scripture passages among Pentecostals. We urge people to experience the baptism in the Holy Spirit, and rightly so. But we have been guilty of making some feel they weren't saved until they received. Maybe we need to stop and ask ourselves why we put such emphasis on the baptism in the Holy Spirit and speaking in tongues. Are our reasons in line with what Jesus intended when He sent the Comforter?

Sometimes I get the feeling we are looking for a security blanket from the Lord. That is wrong. Much emphasis is put on the Baptism as a means to receive power to live overcoming lives. There is a certain validity in that. But why do we want to live overcoming lives? Just to make it easier on us? Just so we can make it into heaven?

An honest look at Acts 1:8 will tell us the purpose of receiving the power of the Holy Spirit is to be witnesses for Jesus. There is no room for doubt left in

Jesus' statement. He simply and emphatically says, "Ye shall be witnesses unto me." There is no question of "wanting to" or "ability." It is to be the response of our lives to the indwelling of the Spirit.

What does it mean to be a witness? A witness is not necessarily one who practices giving testimonials, although this may be a part of it. A witness is one who can no longer be himself, someone has said. He finds himself inhabited by the Holy Spirit of God, whose purpose is to testify of Jesus Christ.

Everything we do and say should bear witness to our relationship with Jesus Christ. If the Holy Spirit is in control our witness will be a positive influence on the lives of those around us.

In leading a neighborhood Bible study we need this added dimension in our lives that only the Holy Spirit can provide. The way we lead the discussion, how we socialize with the group, and the concern we show for their problems all need to be impregnated with His power.

Fruit and Gifts of the Spirit

Being a witness is basically allowing the fruit of the Spirit to grow in our lives until people see a Christlikeness in us. The nine fruit—love, joy, peace, long-suffering, gentleness, goodness, faith, meekness, and temperance—are a vivid description of the character of Jesus. These are the qualities that will draw the non-Christian to Him.

The gifts of the Spirit are also part of our equipment as witnesses. Ray Stedman in his book *Body Life* (Glendale, CA: Regal, 1972) explains that one of the reasons for the manifestation of these gifts is for the work of the ministry to the world. He goes on to say that this ministry should take place out in the world, or out where we meet our non-Christian neighbor face-to-face.

Donald Gee, one of our leading Pentecostal writers, stressed the same concept when he wrote:

> Therefore we must hold fast to rightly understanding the gifts of the Spirit as a divine equipment for the work of World Evangelization. To regard them in any other way is to turn them into a specialty for groups of people that become little more than religious clubs. . . . They are not a hobby to play with; they are tools to work with and weapons to fight with. (Springfield, MO: Gospel Publishing House.)

In leading our Bible study, there were times when my co-leaders and I felt the need of the gift of wisdom to answer challenges to God's Word. We also needed discernment and faith to wait on God to answer our prayers.

We are to "covet earnestly the best gifts," Paul says in 1 Corinthians 12:31. The best gifts, it seems to me, are the ones most needed for the battle we are in at any given moment. But they are available. Along with the Word, which is the Sword of the Spirit, the gifts are our weapons in this spiritual warfare.

We truly need the enabling of the Spirit in our neighborhood Bible study. Without Him we can do nothing.

Are They Hearing What You're Asking?

A lady from another denomination attended Pat's Bible-study group. After listening to the ladies exalt the Lord Jesus during their discussion and sharing time, she told Pat, "I think you folks have something I don't have. I have been in church all my life but I have never been presented with Jesus. I'd like to meet Him."

The purpose of the Bible study was accomplished in that woman's life. The Holy Spirit had enabled Pat and her group to minister in witnessing power, and a soul was born into the kingdom of God.

How did this happen? Eternal truths were communicated in such a way that a desire to know the Author of those truths grew in this woman's heart.

Communication is a much-used word. "But it doesn't sound very spiritual," you may say. And "communication techniques" sounds even less so. Why can't we just say our message and then let the Holy Spirit do the rest? After all, in the last chapter we talked about the necessity of the Spirit's work in the hearts of our non-Christian neighbors.

Along with the firm conviction that we are helpless without the power of the Holy Spirit in our witnessing, I believe God also expects us to use the best methods available to get our message to those who need to hear it. Nothing is really done without some technique guiding it.

Since our responsibility is to communicate truth, we need to know how to do it effectively. First, let's remember, communication is not a one-way radio system—a speaker's message coming over the airwaves with no opportunity for the listener to respond. This is technically a monologue. Small-group Bible studies grow through dialogue. This can be compared to the use of the citizen's band as opposed to the radio. The listener is given an opportunity to respond and react to the Word of God as it is being presented.

Reason for Dialogue

There are at least three basic reasons why dialogue is the best method for presenting the gospel today. First, most non-Christians are relaxed with this approach to religious subjects. Already on the defensive about spiritual matters, they resist being talked to. But many will respond when drawn into dialogue that gives them a chance to express their own opinions.

One of these women was Rose. A neighbor of Phyllis, she was one of the women making candles and discussing personal needs a few days before Phyllis put out the invitation to the Bible study.

"There's got to be more out of life," Rose remembers saying to her friends that day. "We're all happy. We all have good husbands, homes, and children, but something is missing." That conversation was used by the Lord, Rose feels, to prepare them for the call from Phyllis.

When Phyllis called and asked Rose to come to the Bible study, Rose reacted by saying, "Oh, I don't know." But when she heard her friends in the neighborhood were coming, she immediately said,

"Oh, fine, I'll come." As she thought about it later she began to have doubts. She wasn't sure Phyllis would accept her as she was. "What will it be like?" she wondered. But she decided to give it a try.

After coming to the Bible study, she found she enjoyed the discussions. It was something new and exciting. "During those weeks of Bible study," she says, "I realized Jesus had died for me—Rose—and that was so beautiful."

Like many other women in our Bible studies, Rose opened up her heart and mind as she found the dialogue exciting and meaningful.

Dialogue Brings Insight

The second reason for using the discussion method, as opposed to teaching, is the valuable insight it gives the leader about the members' spiritual growth.

The only way to know a person's spiritual needs is to listen to her opinions, questions, and requests. If she remains silent we don't know what set of beliefs she is building her life on. This was especially true in the group I led—a group of well-educated, opinionated women, several of which were members of the cults. Out of our discussions we discovered that one believed in reincarnation, another did not accept the doctrine of the Trinity, and another could not understand what we meant when we used our Christian terminology.

Without this kind of insight into the minds of the members, a group leader may very easily be talking into the air. This has been called the "shotgun" approach—words scattered all over the audience while the teacher hopes something will hit the target of someone's heart.

Observation shows that groups headed by a *teacher* appeal to Christian women. The group may start out with a majority of non-Christians in attendance, but as word gets around that someone is *teaching* a Bible class, Christians rush to fill out the group. As a result, the non-Christians soon disappear. Dialogue with the outsiders breaks down. In using the lecture method, the teacher more often than not misses the questions that originally brought the non-Christians to the group.

Of course, there are times when the Holy Spirit overrules our fumbling efforts and draws a hungry heart to Jesus. The atmosphere of a meeting where the Spirit is in control is contagious and causes many to say, "I want what you've got."

But there are hundreds of thousands (I'm not exaggerating) of women in our neighborhoods who need the opportunity to work through in dialogue their preconceived ideas of what Christians are like and what Christianity is all about.

Ruth was one of these. Living across the street from Bernie, she was naturally invited to Bernie's Bible study. Ruth attended the first meeting along with eight or nine other women. "I was very nervous," she says. "Five or six years previously I had suffered a nervous breakdown, and I didn't know how the ladies would take to me. I didn't know very much about the Bible—hardly anything, really—but the ladies of the Bible study group helped me an awful lot, and at each meeting my heart began to open up to Jesus Christ."

As discussions were led on the Book of Mark, Ruth found not only that she wanted to ask questions concerning the Bible and the Christian experience, but she felt free to ask those questions.

As a result, an awareness of God's truth grew within her. She began to feel different inside. She knew it would be much better if she became a Christian. So, Ruth accepted Jesus as her Saviour and later followed the Lord in water baptism at Calvary Temple, Seattle.

What would have happened if the Bible study had been taught instead of discussed? We can only speculate. What we do know is that Ruth responded to the discussion method. She had questions in her mind and they were answered. The result was her salvation.

Dialogue Brings Understanding

Third, our reason for dialogue is simply that we need to know if what we have said is being understood. We have no way of knowing this without feedback from our listeners. The gospel message needs to be clearly understood. But too often the message sent is not the message received.

There may be a number of reasons for this problem. Possibly we are using language that is not completely understood by the non-Christian. In spite of long usage that has given most words standard meanings, a word may still have a different meaning for different people. This is especially true of abstract words, such as love. Emotional associations collect around these words. People hear what we say and interpret it based on their own experiences.

Though Christian-related terms may sometimes confuse people, we should not discontinue the use of such words as saved, redemption, blessed, faith, and the Kingdom. These words express our beliefs. We should take time to define and explain them. In dialogue we can help people relate the meaning of these words to their own spiritual lives.

Since the purpose of a neighborhood Bible study is evangelistic, this determines the method we use. But none of what I have said negates the method of teaching in certain areas of ministry. Neighborhood evangelism is a specialized ministry and requires special techniques.

Mrs. Harvey Meppelink, a pastor's wife in Everett, Massachusetts, began to lead a Bible study to help several new Christian ladies grow in the Word. These women soon began inviting their friends who later found Jesus Christ as Saviour in the Bible study. Out of this experience, Mrs. Meppelink says, "We make it a rule that we accept a person where she is." Non-Christian neighbors come without the background of spiritual experience and Bible knowledge we are privileged to have. They come with problems and a life-style that may be foreign to us. But before we can effectively communicate with them we have to accept them as they are.

Jesus set the example for us in His ministry. His conversation with the woman at the well in Samaria provides us with a valuable pattern for communicating with a non-Christian.

The first thing we notice about this conversation is how Jesus initiated it. The Samaritan woman was a social outcast in her community, a prostitute. If Jesus had been a conformist He would not have spoken to her at all and society would have approved.

Jesus did not start the conversation with any reference to who she was. Instead, He asked her to do something for Him. That is one way to get a person's attention. It startled the Samaritan woman. Not only was a man speaking to her, but He was a Jew—someone she expected to look down on her because she was a Samaritan.

By initiating the conversation in this way, Jesus was telling the woman that He accepted her as she was. She did not have to change before He would talk with her.

Jesus' acceptance of the Samaritan woman opened up the opportunity to move the conversation into the spiritual realm and to reveal her need as a sinful woman.

When we invite our neighbors to sit down and enter into dialogue with us in Bible study, we are in a real sense asking them to do something for us. We are asking them to share with us something of real value to them—their opinions and ideas—something out of their own thinking. Our neighbors will know we are accepting them as they are.

It is so easy for the non-Christian to feel we have a holier-than-thou attitude, even when we don't. They are very aware and sensitive to our different life-style. We don't partake of some of the things they do. Often they believe we subscribe to a religion of "don'ts." So we need to do something positive to convince them we want to communicate with them. Making them feel they can give something to us can do that.

For this reason, in a neighborhood Bible study asking, not telling, is one of the communication techniques we use. Many believe that communication is accomplished simply by telling people what they ought to know and then leaving it up to them what they do with it. They will probably forget most of it. Educators tell us we forget 90 percent of what we hear, but we remember 90 percent of what we say.

We want the Word of God to speak to our group members. We want the Holy Spirit to communicate with them. This can take place when the leader throws out questions that keep the women looking into the Word for the answers.

Listening Is Important

Our ultimate goal is to communicate people's need of a Saviour. But sometimes we have to begin with their need to be listened to, their need to find answers for problems in their family, their need to be loved by another human being. Then, like Jesus, we can use those needs to whet their curiosity about the gift of God. When their curiosity is aroused it is only a step further to sharing spiritual truths.

When people see we are interested in them, they are more likely to become interested in our Lord. This requires emotional involvement. It takes patience to hear people out. But listening tells people we want to understand them. When we have listened to them, it is more likely they will listen to the Lord.

There are always shy ones in every group. The good leader will be alert to opportunities to get them to express themselves in the discussion. She will make them feel their contribution is needed by the group.

It is important that everyone be given a chance to speak at each meeting. However, if someone tells us through her posture, facial expression, or any other nonverbal communication that she isn't ready to talk, she shouldn't be forced to say anything.

Sometimes there is the other extreme—the person who talks excessively. She may have to be dealt with in love outside the meeting. She will need to be made aware that others also have a right to share in the discussion and no one person can be allowed to monopolize it.

Often women attend our groups who are totally overwhelmed with their problems. Jane was one of these when she began to attend Pat's Bible study. Her life was immersed in problems and she felt like she was drowning. As she talked out of a troubled heart, Pat listened and then prayed with her.

Again and again Jane came back, reaching back into her childhood to reveal all the injuries life had handed her. Pat listened and searched and prayed for ways to help this desperate woman.

Jane had been through analysis but hadn't been helped. Now she had turned to Pat and the Bible study. After listening for some time to repeated recitals of Jane's problems, Pat realized she needed to be firm with her.

"We're not going to give you permission to state that again," Pat told her one day when Jane started to restate her problems. Pat says, "We had to come to the point of change deliberately. Then she began to listen and to change."

Jane did listen and turned herself and her problems over to the Lord. Today she is a different woman.

Women will join a Bible-study group who have a message of their own they want to give out. From time to time they will attempt to lead the discussion off on a tangent. After attending a Bible study for a few weeks, one woman interrupted the discussion one afternoon to tell everyone, "I am glad I believe I'll be able to come back to life again after I die. That way I will be able to make up for the wrong things I do now."

The group was shocked into silence. The Christians in the group began to pray for the wisdom of the Lord in answering this comment. The leader felt led to quietly and quickly explain that she believed Jesus died for those sins so we could be forgiven now. Everyone relaxed and the discussion on the Scripture passage for that meeting continued.

In 2 Timothy 2:14, 16, and 23 Paul gives advice that every leader needs to follow in leading discussions:

> Of these things put them in remembrance, charging them before the Lord that they strive not about words to no profit, but to the subverting of the hearers. . . .

> But shun profane and vain babblings: for they will increase unto more ungodliness.... But foolish and unlearned questions avoid, knowing that they do gender strife.

Spiritual growth never occurs by trying to deal with all the tangents people will veer off on. Most are vain babbling or unlearned questions.

What if someone has a serious question but it is not on the subject being discussed? Such questions should always be answered. If possible, the leader should meet with the one who asked it after the discussion is concluded.

Communicate Content

Another example Jesus left us was the way He handled the content of the gospel. He did not reduce the plan of salvation to a simple step-by-step outline and hand it to everyone He met. Jesus dealt with individuals and He communicated with them on their particular level of understanding and need.

Both in the area of getting into a right relationship with God and in the blessed results, Jesus applied His teachings to the person. The Samaritan woman had to learn to worship God in truth and to repent of her immoral life. Jesus promised her living water so she would never thirst again. Jesus told Nicodemus he had to be born again to see the kingdom of God.

As we lead people to discover God's truth let us emphasize the good gifts of God along with the need for repentance. No matter what it may cost a woman to give her life to God, the benefits are greater. Like Jesus, we must show our neighbors how God's blessings will benefit them in areas of their particular needs.

Communication is basically the art or ability to transmit a message. It requires a sender and a receiver, In a Christian evangelistic Bible study the discussion method is the leader's tool, and its use should bring understanding of God's Word, accompanied by changed attitudes.

7

Do They Know You Care?

Shirley came to our very first meeting of the neighborhood Bible study I agreed to lead for Alma. She sat on the sofa holding her 18-month-old son on her lap. Her dark hazel eyes shone as she listened intently to Inga's story.

Shirley didn't say much that day or in the weeks to follow, but she continued to come. The first time we realized she wasn't agreeing with us was in the middle of a discussion on faith. Breaking in with antagonism in her voice, she asked, "What is faith?" We briefly explained how faith is an integral part of everyday living and then continued with our study in the Word.

Later that fall, it became evident that Shirley was having emotional problems. Her surroundings, people, and events became distorted in her mind. One day when she was sharing some of this with me, I asked if she would pray with me.

"I can't pray," she answered. "I'm a product of the scientific age."

We soon learned that she called herself an agnostic, declaring she didn't know what sin is. Her husband claimed to be an atheist. Yet she continued to attend our weekly Bible study, and a burden for her grew in our hearts.

By Thanksgiving, Shirley was in the hospital. We Christians in the group had been praying for her healing. Instead of the miracle we desired, God gave us an opportunity to care for her. As she was in and out of the hospital during that holiday season, different ones in the group provided for the family. Some cleaned her house; others baby-sat with the two boys. Food was taken in and a floral arrangement sent for Christmas.

We visited her in the hospital and our pastor did also. Once I happened to call on her right after our pastor had been there. She eagerly told me how he had prayed with her and how she felt so much better.

But still our prayers for complete healing were not answered. Over the next 5 years, from time to time, the Christians in that neighborhood showed Shirley and her family the love of God in action.

The result is that today Shirley is fully trusting the Lord for her eternal salvation and her health. She calls me occasionally to tell me she prays and reads her Bible daily. And when I speak at conferences she is one of those praying for me. This is the woman who a few years ago said, "I can't pray."

Caring Is Essential

Not all Bible-study groups will have to work so hard at caring for one of its members. Yet caring is essential to communicating the message of God's love to our non-Christian neighbors.

It is best accomplished by meeting our neighbors at their point of physical or emotional need. Jesus did this. He met the Samaritan woman's need for social acceptance first. This opened the way for meeting her spiritual need.

Another woman broke an alabaster box of ointment to anoint Jesus' feet after washing them with her tears and wiping them with her hair. Others would have turned her away, but Jesus cared and He accepted her attention.

He met the physical need of the woman who had an "issue of blood twelve years" by healing her first and then giving her spiritual comfort. Other examples could be given, such as the blind man sitting by the road to Jericho and the woman bent over double whom Jesus healed in the synagogue on the Sabbath. These show us that caring for people's physical and emotional needs can be a way to reveal God's love to them.

Sometimes in our busyness we forget we are representatives of Christ in this world. But the non-Christian does not forget what claims we make when we call ourselves Christians. Just as Jesus went about doing good, they expect us to do the same.

The saddest, most regrettable experience I've ever had was when I failed to care for a non-Christian with whom I had worked hard at developing a friendship. I was too busy with my own affairs and failed to visit her husband while he was in the hospital recovering from a heart attack. By the time I got around to calling on the phone, he was home and she had decided I didn't really care after all. I wept bitterly and it has taken several years to even begin rebuilding that friendship.

Why do I feel so strongly about this? Because as far as I know I am the only Christian friend this person has. And according to God's Word my responsibility is to be a minister of reconciliation to her.

Not Always Convenient

From my experience I learned that caring is not

always convenient. Jesus sat down at the well in Samaria to rest, but the need to care for a lonely woman interrupted His rest. He was interrupted in the middle of a dinner party, on a journey, in a synagogue service, and in the middle of a crowd, but He always responded to the individual's need.

It was seldom convenient when Shirley telephoned and said, "I need you." At times like that, our commitment to Jesus Christ requires that we respond to the individual in need. Because the Christians in her neighborhood responded in love, Shirley was able to eventually lift her hands and her heart heavenward and say, "Father, I need You, save me."

Our most powerful wedge into the lives of others is simply being able to love as Christ loves. This is really what transforms—not doctrine or ethics, but loving deeds. Not even group communication techniques (in spite of spending a whole chapter on them), but Christian caring. Communication techniques are important but if they are not impregnated with a caring attitude they can be sterile and fruitless. If the caring is there it will bring life to the communication.

We had been meeting for some months when Suzanne invited Carol to attend. Carol came and freely entered into our discussions. After the first meeting she told Suzanne she had never before been in a group where she felt such warmth and acceptance.

A few weeks later, she asked us to pray with her and in tears told us the doctors had discovered her 9-year-old son had a defective heart. We prayed at the meeting and continued to do so during the following weeks.

About a month later, Carol reported to the group that after careful examination at the orthopedic hospital, the doctor decided her son would not need open-heart surgery. We gave God the glory.

Carol went back to work in her husband's office a few weeks later and could not continue to attend our meetings. We felt God had given her to us for that short time so we could care for her need. This episode also witnessed to the non-Christians in the group of God's power and love.

Caring Involvement

Caring demands involvement with other people—the kind of involvement that gives warm support. This requires that we know something about them—about their past, their present, and their future.

To really know people we need to know a little of their history. Where have they come from? What events and people in their past have shaped their lives? We also need to know what's happening to them in the present. What interests do they have? What about their families? And then we need to know something of their dreams and goals for the future.

All this can be explored during the few minutes of socializing over a cup of coffee after they arrive and just before the Bible study begins. To be interested in another person to this extent breaks down many barriers and makes it easier to share the gospel. This is part of building that bridge of friendship we talked about in chapter 2.

As we move into the Bible study itself we show we care for the individuals in our group through our attitude. If we feel we have all the answers or that we ourselves are going to meet their needs, we will accomplish nothing more than putting the women on the defensive.

Honesty before God requires that we admit we don't have all the answers. Nobody does. Only God does. Nor are we able to meet every need. But we can be of assistance to them. What they need is for us to point the way to God who can meet their needs.

We can do this by several means. As we emphasized in the last chapter, we can listen to them. Everyone needs to be listened to. This tells people we are 100 percent available to them.

With today's pressures and anxieties, it is becoming harder to get someone to stop long enough to listen. Everyone has her own set of problems. Who has time or strength to add someone else's worries to her own heavy load? Could this be the reason psychologists are so much in demand? Are we in a situation where we have to pay to be listened to? What an opportunity we Christians have for caring!

One of the benefits of listening is the leader can find things to affirm in the members of her group. Not only do people need to be listened to, but they also need to know they are worthwhile. To respond positively to something someone has said, to give an honest compliment, or just to say, "I appreciate you and your contribution," will show that person she counts with you. And you will be a long way down the road to influencing her for righteousness.

Caring Through Prayer

Prayer is one of the most effective tools we have for caring. I have always closed each meeting with a time for taking the needs of the members before God. And when the answers come in, as in Carol's case, the group learns through experience that God cares too.

I usually open up the prayer time to conversational prayer, saying that anyone who wants to pray should feel free to do so. I begin myself to set the example. We must remember that the very first prayer the leader prays will set the prayer pattern for the rest of the time. If I as a leader pray a long, drawn-out prayer using all the theological phrases I know, I will scare off any non-Christian and probably many Christians from ever becoming involved in the prayer time. So I encourage short sentence prayers.

"Wait a minute," I hear you say. "Ask non-Christians to pray?" Yes, I invite anyone present to join me in praying. I am aware that some of them need to pray the sinner's prayer before praying for a sick neighbor, but who knows what may happen between them and the Lord as they direct their minds and, hopefully, their hearts heavenward during those few minutes we spend in prayer? Those are serious minutes and their hearts may be more receptive then than during our whole hour of discussion. It may well be the time the Holy Spirit will be able to speak in convincing power to them. Because I care, I want to give them every opportunity to respond to Him.

Also, because I care I have learned to be careful about prayer requests. I find that as the women begin to know each other more intimately, some of the prayer requests gradually become opportunities for sharing bits of neighborhood gossip. By using conversational prayer it isn't necessary to go through the procedure of taking requests and the temptation to say too much is eliminated.

I have also found that as the group grows in closeness, the members freely share their needs with each other in general conversation. Sometimes this happens before or after the hour of Bible study. Sometimes it occurs during the week between the meetings.

One of our most important rules in an evangelistic Bible study is that we never carry confidences outside the group. To have a member share some intimate detail of her life in her search for help is a very serious matter. If this information finds its way into the other homes in the neighborhood, our credibility and Christian witness suffers. Again, because we care we take these needs to our Heavenly Father only.

Much of the caring ministry in a Bible study is done throughout the week between meetings. Prayer is an essential part of that ministry. As a leader, I pray for each member of the group by name every week. As I learn to know them individually and their needs and personal desires, I pray specifically for these needs.

It is invaluable to have one or two Christian co-workers in the group. My co-workers prayed with me for the women and for the success of the Friday afternoon meetings. Sometimes when the needs were overwhelming, we agreed to set aside a certain day of the week to fast and pray individually in our own homes. Other times we Christians met together for an hour once a week just to pray for our non-Christian members.

We saw God answer many of these prayers in miraculous ways. The real turning point came in Shirley's life when several of us agreed to pray together.

We took Jesus' words literally when He said: "If two of you shall agree on earth as touching any thing that they shall ask, it shall be done for them of my Father which is in heaven" (Matthew 18:19).

We decided that whatever we were doing every day when the clock said noon, we would stop and pray for a minute for Shirley. We did this for almost 2 months one summer when she seemed to be at her lowest. Before the summer was over she was well again and had committed her heart and life fully to the Lord. That was the breakthrough we had desired and prayed for all those years.

Qualities in Caring

Researchers in the field of psychology have determined there are three qualities needed in persons who are caring for or helping others. These are empathy, warmth, and genuineness.

Empathy is sensitivity to the current feelings of another person. We have to let that neighbor know we understand her feelings in whatever situation she is in. Sometimes we have to stretch our own thinking and feelings with a prayer for compassion. But if we can enter into another's feelings and experiences she will know we are with her in her struggle. She will believe we care and it will be easier to convince her God cares.

Warmth means accepting another person just as she is. It is an in-spite-of-not-deserving-it love, without being condescending. Isn't that the way God loves us? Can any of us say we deserve to be loved by the Lord? This warmth does not impose any conditions on the other person. Her uniqueness and individuality are accepted and valued.

Warmth comes through in our actions more clearly than our words. How we respond with facial expression, gestures, eye-contact, or any other nonverbal behavior expresses our warmth or our lack of it. When warmth is present it says, "I care."

Genuineness is the ability to know and be true to oneself. It requires complete honesty about ourselves. Anything less produces a certain amount of phoniness. Genuineness means being free but consistent about values and in attitudes. When we are genuine we are not on the defensive. It gets rid of professionalism and let's my neighbor know "this is the real me who cares."

Whoever your neighbor is she needs the gifts of these qualities from you. Whatever her physical, emotional, or spiritual need, God needs you to care for her. You may very well be the only Christian who does care.

The Bible Study and the Family

Lois, a graduate of Julliard School of Music, moved to Alma's neighborhood only a few months before we began the neighborhood Bible study. She had attended a Bible study in the city where she had lived before moving to the suburbs. Anxious to get into another group, Lois was one of the original five women who met in Alma's home to plan the Bible study.

We did not realize at that first meeting how often we would be called on to minister, not only to Lois but to her family as well. But we were pleased when she suggested we use her home for the neighborhood tea we planned to give the next week. When she offered the use of her home, she half-apologized for its not being finished yet.

Lois' husband Lou was having the house built, taking a special interest in it, and even doing some of the work himself. Designed like an English cottage with dark wood, beamed ceilings, and a copper hood over the fireplace, it looked like a house in one of Charles Dickens' novels. Lou also took time to attend antique auctions to find the furniture he wanted for the house. Then one day he told Lois, "This house will lend itself very well to a seance." Lou had been attending spiritualism meetings.

During this time, their son Roger was attending the university where he was introduced to drugs by a psychology professor. Roger began to use the drugs heavily and then to study the eastern religions.

Lois says, "During this period, the Bible study helped me keep my sanity. It was so heartbreaking."

The Christians in the group took Lois' burdens before the Lord in prayer. We set aside days to fast and pray and we saw God answer those prayers. At one point Lou scheduled a seance to be held in their home. We prayed that week with Lois and at the next Bible study she reported that the seance had been canceled.

We also prayed for Roger. About the middle of the school year, Roger returned home to live. He was broken in spirit and destitute physically. As we prayed for him, Lois took him to church. She also took him to visit the leader of the Bible study she had previously attended. This woman prayed for Roger and counseled him about his spiritual life. For a while Roger attended the youth group at Calvary Temple. Then he found a job in Alaska where he began attending an Assembly of God. God had answered our prayers.

Recently he wrote the following to his father:

> On the eve of my birthday I wish to share some thoughts from my heart. I feel a deep need for reconciliation, and I want to affirm my responsibilities and dedication to you. This letter is made possible by the saving grace of Christ and the power which the Name of Jesus has to work miracles and change lives.

Roger experienced this miracle-working power in his life because a group of women in a Bible study were burdened for the family of one of their members.

Salvation for Families

In Acts 16 we find Paul ministering to the jailor who had guarded him and Silas in their prison confinement. When the jailor cried out, "What must I do to be saved?" they answered, "Believe on the Lord Jesus Christ, and thou shalt be saved, and thy house" (vv. 30, 31).

How could Paul and Silas make such a promise? We know that husbands and children do not automatically receive salvation because a wife and mother believes. Salvation is a personal, not a group, experience. But it is dependent on belief, which is made possible by hearing the gospel. Husbands and children have to hear the gospel for themselves.

In this light it is significant that Acts 16:32-34 records the following:

> And they spake unto him the word of the Lord, and to all that were in his house. And he took them the same hour of the night, and washed their stripes; and was baptized, he and all his, straightway. And when he had brought them into his house, he set meat before them, and rejoiced, believing in God with all his house.

When the jailor saw the power of God in action, he spontaneously cried out for his life. It is significant that Paul and Silas included the jailor's family in their response. The principle is true for our neighborhood Bible studies. Our job is not completed until we have given the families an opportunity as well.

When Paul and Silas were given the chance to speak to the jailor's family, the family believed the gospel message as well, and when the jailor was baptized so were those in his house. That is the pattern we desire for all our Bible studies.

Sometimes, as in the story of Lois, the women in

our groups will open the way for us to minister to their families through prayer and witnessing. In other cases, husbands will become curious about what has happened to their wives and they will begin to ask questions. This can lead to developing groups for couples.

Ministering to Family Members

We who lead Bible studies must be alert to ways to involve families in activities that tie them in with the Bible study. One natural ministry closely associated with the Bible study is baby-sitting. Children need to be cared for while the mothers are meeting in the group. But it can be much more than just a baby-sitting service. The time can be used to share the love of God with those children through stories and songs.

In our Bible study, we found it advantageous to meet in a different home each week. It not only deepened the commitment of the women to the group, but it also got the study of the Word into homes where the Bible probably hadn't been dusted off for years. The children in the home became aware their mother was studying the Bible.

This may sound like I am stretching the value of a Bible study to the family. But we must remember that before people—children and adults alike—can make a decision for Jesus Christ they have to be confronted with the seriousness of His life and claims. There must be an awareness of God before revival can occur. And in our culture today it is entirely possible for people to go through days, weeks, and months without thinking of God or being confronted with His existence.

Sundays are spent in front of the television set, in the mountains, or at the lake. Christmas is deprived of all religious significance in public schools. Christmas programs are now "holiday" programs. Easter is sold out to the rabbit family, egg hunts, and spring fashions. In our society, if a family is not attending church, where will their children become aware that God and the Bible are more than an ancient myth?

In Romans 10:13, 14, Paul writes:

> For whosoever shall call upon the name of the Lord shall be saved. How then shall they call on him in whom they have not believed? and how shall they believe in him of whom they have not heard? and how shall they hear without a preacher?

This is Paul's line of logic. The offer of salvation is to everyone. But only those who hear it can accept the offer and believe. Our responsibility is to give everyone we possibly can a chance to hear. By expanding our vision of the ministry of a Bible study to include the families of the women in our groups, we can give more people a chance to hear.

In an earlier chapter we related the story of Donna who went home from the Bible study and began to win her own children to the Lord—one by one until she had won all seven. Then she went on to minister to the school-age children of the neighborhood, many of whom were children of the women who attended our Bible study.

Involving Our Own Families

During this time, Alma's son Wayne, who was a student at the university, became concerned about the teenagers in the neighborhood. He started a small-group Bible study for them. Before it ended he was able to lead one of the girls to the Lord, a daughter of one of our women in the study group.

We were concerned about the husbands of the women in our Bible study. We not only prayed for them, we also put on a potluck supper about twice a year for our husbands. We felt they should be more aware of what we women were doing and also be given a chance to become acquainted with the Christian husbands. At one of the potlucks (as mentioned in an earlier chapter) we showed a film on the Holy Land. To this film had been added narration that clearly presented the gospel message. Each of the husbands heard it that night.

Probably one of the greatest satisfactions to come out of leading a neighborhood Bible study is to see the involvement of your own family. My husband was my prayer partner. He took it on himself, as did Alma's husband, to show a personal interest in Shirley's husband. As couples, we included Shirley and her husband in various church activities.

Our children became involved. Alma's son actually led a group for his peers. Some of our daughters helped with baby-sitting during vacation times. It brought joy to my heart on the days of our study to hear my own daughters say, "Mother, I'll pray for you today."

When someone in the group would call asking for help, my family took it for granted I would respond. On one occasion when I didn't respond fast enough, one of my daughters impatiently said, "Mother, aren't you going to help her?"

The memories of the struggles and prayers, but especially of the victories of that Bible study, are a part of my daughters' heritage. They know God lives and works miracles today because they learned to know those people and saw changes in their lives.

The best way to insure our children's spiritual growth is to let them have a part in a ministry to others and to let them see for themselves God's power at work in the lives of spiritually destitute people.

The Bible Study and the Church

One Sunday afternoon several years ago I walked into the fireside room of the Assembly of God in Port Angeles, Washington, and was greeted by an excited group of women. Their enthusiasm was aflame with the thrill of having seen God at work in their community through neighborhood Bible studies.

The vision had been born about a year before when Pastor Frank Cole and his wife Jean attended a seminar in southern California that presented the concept of lay ministries in the church. That same fall at the Northwest District Women's Ministries retreat a panel of women from the Seattle area told about their experiences in neighborhood Bible studies.

One of the laywomen, Patty, from Port Angeles, attended that retreat also. The idea for such an evangelistic outreach in their own community was planted in both Jean's and Patty's hearts.

Burdened for two women who had been friends of hers before her conversion, Patty felt God wanted her to witness for Him in this way. With the encouragement of the Coles, she contacted others simply by knocking on doors.

A group of 10 women came together, and Patty knew God had given them to her. But there were times when she became discouraged. As the weeks went by some of the women weren't always faithful, and Patty began to doubt that she really should be doing this. But the Coles continued to encourage her.

Patty soon discovered she needed to build bridges of friendship during the week between meetings. This required involvement in their lives, plus hours of intercessory prayer—an investment of time and energy.

Her desire was not just to lead the group in an hour of discussion each week, but rather to lead them into a relationship with Jesus Christ. As she got better acquainted with the women, she took Jean with her to visit them in their homes. One by one they were introduced to the pastor's wife in this way. But Jean never sat in on the Bible study. Both Jean and Patty felt that Jean's presence would frighten the women, most of whom were not church-goers at this time.

God began to answer Patty's prayers. One morning as she was leading the study in John 4 concerning the woman at the well, she noticed a look of surprise on the face of one woman. Patty felt impressed of the Holy Spirit that Louise was ready to accept the Lord.

That afternoon she knew she must go to Louise's home. Somewhat frightened by the challenge, Patty drove past the house, but she could not shake the feeling that she had to go back. When she went to the door, Louise answered her knock with, "I was just praying the Lord would send you." That afternoon a soul was born into Christ's kingdom.

Another woman came to the Lord in much the same manner. Others were saved when they were brought to church and still others were saved in Patty's home. In a year's time all 10 women became Christians.

A Second Group—And a Third

About this time another young woman, Sonja, also

felt led to begin a study group in her home. Sonja was concerned about numerous friends and neighbors, but especially about the residents in a duplex next door. In an adventure of faith, she claimed that duplex and its occupants for the Lord.

One of these was a young woman whose marriage was crumbling. Judy had a deep spiritual need, and Sonja was able to share Christ and His love with her. Gradually bridges were built, and Judy was ready to accept when asked to join a Bible-study group. Two months later she yielded her life to Christ.

Sonja discontinued the study during the summer. As fall drew near, she really did not want to become involved again. But she prayed, "Lord, show me." Not long after this, Judy called and said, "I have a new member for the group." This removed all doubt about starting again.

A third group was started by a Sunday school teacher, Dorothy. She became burdened for the mother of one of her students. Faye had explored the cults, attended seances, and finally in desperation prayed, "If there is a God, send somebody to my door." That day, Dorothy came.

After Faye's conversion, Dorothy felt led to begin a home Bible study to strengthen Faye in her newfound faith. It was not long until Faye brought two of her friends.

One of these women, Betty, came only out of friendship and showed little response to the gospel. But consistent love and prayer finally broke her resistance and she gave her heart to the Lord.

Eight months after Betty was saved, she and her 2-year-old son were killed in an auto accident. But because someone started a home Bible study, Betty is in heaven today.

These home Bible studies did not leave out the

men. As the women found Christ and talked of their new joy at home, the husbands began to ask questions about what was happening to their wives.

When this happened Patty invited each couple individually to her home for coffee and dessert on a Friday evening. She and her husband Leon united in this effort. Invariably the evening's conversation led into a discussion of spiritual values. Out of this developed a group for couples that met on Friday evenings. Leon led these studies, and many of the husbands found Jesus as Saviour in Patty and Leon's living room.

During this period, the Coles remained in the background as far as the actual studies went. But they continued to pray for the leaders and to encourage and counsel them in this evangelistic outreach.

As the number of new converts multiplied, the need to tie them in with the church became apparent. Pastor Cole organized a pastor's class to meet during the midweek service. This seemed to be the most convenient time for most of the new converts to attend.

Each class met for 7 weeks. Pastor Cole instructed them in the assurance of salvation, the Christian warfare, the church ordinances, fundamental doctrines, and their relationship to the church.

During these sessions new converts were encouraged to share their testimony of salvation. This prepared them for witnessing to their unsaved relatives and friends.

They shared their problems too and at the same time learned to support each other in prayer. A bond of unity in the Lord developed during those sessions and the fellowship of the new converts was grounded in the church.

About a year and a half after the first Bible study began, 22 new converts had been added to the Port

Angeles Assembly because of neighborhood Bible studies.

More Bible Studies

A period of nurturing the new converts in the fellowship of the church followed. They found their places of service and were encouraged and strengthened in their faith through special classes. Then about 2 years ago, Jean felt it was time to move out into the community again with the gospel message. New Bible-study groups were formed.

Jean prayed that God would speak to the people who should be involved. She was willing to coordinate the groups but the leader of each group would have to be a laywoman in the church.

Because Jean was desirous of allowing God to lead the women of the church into this ministry, she extended an open invitation to anyone interested in starting a neighborhood Bible study. They were invited to a meeting at the church. She also asked for volunteer baby-sitters. At this meeting Jean presented the Bible-study guide *Looking at Jesus With Luke*, and instructed the potential leaders in how to use it.

After that Jean met with them once a month. They shared their victories and brought their prayer requests. They supported each other in the ministry God had given them. The meeting was always open to anyone who was interested in a neighborhood ministry.

Four Bible studies were organized soon after the first meeting. They all met in different homes throughout the community but on the same day. The associate pastor's wife, Cathy Hagen, and two new converts volunteered to care for the children at the church. Cathy and her helpers prepared Bible stories and activities for the children. They wanted it to be more than just a baby-sitting service. Their efforts were more than rewarded when the mothers returned to pick up their children. Many walked in with tears of joy on their cheeks and a new radiance in their eyes. God had done a work of salvation or blessing in their lives and the baby-sitters were the first to hear them tell of it.

Also under Jean's supervision, the Women's Ministries leader, Lillian, led a study on the Holy Spirit on another day of the week. Many of the women attended both. Six women were baptized in the Spirit during this period.

As a result of the four groups reaching out to their non-Christian neighbors, eight women were saved. One of the leaders, Sonja, says, "Older Christians lose contact with people in the world. It takes something like this to make us reach out and invite the non-Christian to hear the gospel."

Jean Cole believes any church whose women will venture out into neighborhood Bible studies is a church that will see revival. Over the past 5 years she says 60 people have been saved as a result of the neighborhood Bible studies, some directly, others through new converts bringing their friends to church. That is part of the unending story of the influence of the gospel through a neighborhood evangelism program in one church.

Go to the People

The story of the Port Angeles church is not totally unique. God is moving across the country to reach non-Christians in much the same way. As pastors find that the unsaved of their communities do not come eagerly to announced evangelistic services, they are moving their efforts out into the neighborhoods where the people are.

Jesus indicated the necessity of this approach in the story in Luke 14:16-24. A man had prepared a banquet and sent out invitations, only to have the intended guests give all kinds of excuses for not being able to attend. In response, the host told his servants to go out and invite others to come to the banquet. They were instructed to go to two different areas:

> Go out quickly into the streets and lanes of the city, and bring in hither the poor, and the maimed, and the halt, and the blind. . . . Go out into the highways and hedges, and compel them to come in, that my house may be filled (vv. 21, 23).

Most Bible scholars feel this parable deals with the Jews' rejection of God's invitation to accept His Son Jesus, and the extending of the invitation then to the Gentiles. I don't think it is a misinterpretation to note that when the invited guests would not respond to the invitation, the servants were sent *out* to *find* others to enjoy the banquet.

I think we all recognize that mass evangelism is not as effective today as it was 50 to 100 years ago. There was a time when a special speaker with an exciting title for a sermon would pack a church out. Altar calls would be given and many people would walk the long aisle to the front. For years during my childhood and teens, I remember seeing someone, sometimes several people, at the altar for salvation after every Sunday morning and every Sunday evening service.

This is not happening today to that extent. Yet people *are* getting saved. And our churches are growing. The methods have changed. One of the methods blessed of God today is the sending out of laypersons into their own neighborhoods.

It is important that neighborhood evangelism efforts be promoted and supported by local churches. Independent groups springing up in neighborhoods do not meet the full needs of our neighbors. The ultimate goal of a Bible study should be to lead the women into the church where they can become involved in the fellowship of other Christians and receive the pastoral care and guidance they need.

Church-based Evangelism

When the disciples, after the Day of Pentecost, obeyed Jesus' command to make more disciples, Luke wrote: "And the Lord added to the church daily such as should be saved" (Acts 2:47).

It is apparent it is God's plan for new converts to become a part of the church body. God wants our churches to grow. This in turn provides a stronger base for more evangelism. As the process becomes a cycle of church growth through church-based evangelism, God will be glorified through an ever enlarging community of Christians. This is our purpose.

The neighborhood Bible study is not meant to take the place of the church. It is an arm of the church, extending out into the neighborhoods. As converts are made, they should be added to the church as they were in the days of the apostles. The church is where the new converts will find not only fellowship but also a place of service. Under the guidance of the pastor they will grow in their spiritual life. The neighborhood Bible study is evangelistic—a halfway house, standing between the world and the church.

If I understand Paul's teaching in Ephesians 4:11, 12, everyone who becomes a Christian needs a pastor's ministry. "And he [Christ] gave ... pastors and teachers; for the perfecting of the saints, for the work of the ministry, for the edifying of the body of Christ."

For this reason, we bring new converts from the Bible studies into the local church. But occasionally there is someone like Betty who became a Christian in Dorothy's group in Port Angeles. Betty's husband would not allow her to attend church at all. The Bible study was her source of spiritual encouragement and instruction. But because the Bible study was a part of the Port Angeles church's outreach, Dorothy and Faye brought Pastor Cole to Betty when they could not bring her to him. He became her pastor.

In my own experience as a lay leader, I have found I needed my pastor for guidance in my involvement with a neighborhood Bible study. When a question arose that I did not have the answer for, he became my resource person. When I was fighting the spiritual battle for the salvation of a lost soul, he became my prayer partner. And he was a constant source of encouragement in my weekly commitment to go out on the front line of the battle.

As a result, my pastor and my church became more important to me than ever before. I looked forward with new anticipation to the church services. They were my source of refreshing and instruction, a means of building up my own inner strength.

I have seen this happen in other women as they became involved in neighborhood evangelism. One woman expressed her enthusiasm by saying, "I wish everyone could do this. Our church would be revitalized."

Do you want revival in your church? Pastors, encourage your laypeople to get involved in neighborhood evangelism.

10

Joy in Neighborhood Evangelism

Nothing compares with the joy of leading a lost, searching neighbor into a living relationship with our Saviour, Jesus Christ. Joy is experienced by both the Christian and the new convert. It is so like the joy of welcoming a new baby into the house. Parents, brothers and sisters, grandparents, aunts and uncles all glow and respond to the excitement of a new life in the home. And the family of God experiences a similar, yet deeper, joy when a new babe in Christ is born into life everlasting.

This happens over and over in neighborhood Bible studies. It happened in the life of Joyce and the group she attended.

A young, attractive brunette in her early thirties, Joyce radiates a peace of heart as she talks convincingly of her relationship with the Lord. But it hasn't always been this way.

The daughter of parents who suffered an unhappy and broken marriage, Joyce was reluctant to marry until in her middle twenties when she met a man she felt sure she loved and who loved her. None of his relatives attended their wedding, but she rationalized that they probably disapproved of their having a civil ceremony.

Joyce was not to be happily married for long. In just a few months she discovered her husband had committed bigamy, having a wife and children in another part of the state. When the first wife refused to divorce him, Joyce sought legal advice. They were in the process of untangling their problems when her husband died of a massive coronary.

Summing up those tragic events, she says, "It was the most horrible year and a half you could ever have."

Loving to dance, and not seeing anything wrong with drinking, Joyce turned to pleasure as a way of blotting out the past. And wherever there was dancing there was drinking, until Joyce says drinking became her life-style.

At the same time, she was fascinated by Ouija boards and palm and card reading. As she got more involved in these forms of the occult, she felt there was a power in them. Not knowing much about the Bible, she attributed that power to God.

Her main interest was in astrology. She thought it would help her understand herself and others. She was impressed with its prophecies and their fulfillment. She began to wonder about the existence of a devil but doubted there was such a personality. All this time she had a strong feeling of searching for something.

At an all-day seminar she was introduced to the power of the occult, beginning with astrology, palm reading, people with psychic abilities, handwriting analysis, taro card reading, and supernatural inscriptions on walls—the whole community of the occult world. For several months after that she commuted to another town to attend a home class on palm reading. As she continued this study she became frightened, living in fear that some of the dire predictions would come true.

Her attitude toward life became pessimistic. She was on the verge of panic most of the time, waiting for the worst to happen. She was afraid to face every new day. She had no peace, just pressure. And she was always hoping but never received any satisfaction. It affected her relationships with other people. She began to wonder if she was losing her mind or being overpowered.

Then she met and fell in love with the man who is now her husband. They were married and she quit attending the home classes in palm reading. Shortly after that someone gave her a copy of *The Late Great Planet Earth*. She became fascinated with it and the book remained on her mind for a couple of years. Also, a fellow worker at her office began sharing with her about the *PTL Club*.

In the meantime, her sister Louise began attending a neighborhood Bible study led by an Assemblies of God pastor's wife. Louise reported to Joyce the questions and discussions at the weekly meetings. Joyce became so interested that after she quit work, she began to attend on Friday mornings.

"I really enjoyed the fellowship and getting my questions answered," she says. The group was studying the life of Christ at the time and Joyce had many questions on her heart. Although, as the leader recalls, Joyce was not very talkative at first, the Lord was faithful in providing the answers she was searching for. They were answered through the discussions out of the Word of God.

Joyce was very teachable. At one of the Bible studies, she was asked to read Acts 19:18-20—the story of the burning of the books in Ephesus. Joyce went home that day and destroyed all the things connected with the occult she had, even a set of mugs with the signs of the Zodiac on them.

A few weeks later she attended a Sunday evening service at the Assembly of God in her community. When the altar call was given, Joyce went forward.

She says, "Going forward meant I was saying, 'Jesus, take control of my life. I repent of my sins. I've had control; now I'll do things Your way.'"

Joyce wept that night—tears of repentance, but also tears of joy. She says, "When I left the church that night I experienced the peace and serenity of the Holy Spirit. It was the most beautiful thing I have ever experienced."

The years of searching, questioning, and torment were over for Joyce. She was now a new creation in Christ Jesus and the joy of salvation was hers.

Since then she has also experienced the joy of seeing someone she loves come to know Jesus—her own mother.

God used a neighborhood Bible study to lead Joyce into the kingdom of God. A new member was added to the local church, and through her another needy soul—her mother—was reached and also added to the local church.

This kind of growth brings true and everlasting joy both to the new convert and to those who have helped her find the Lord. This is the glorious result of all the hours, energy, and money spent in taking the gospel to our neighbors.

How to Start a Neighborhood Bible Study

By now I hope you are asking, "How and when can I get involved in a neighborhood Bible study?"

In preceding chapters I tried to relate some of the challenges as well as the joys and rewards of neighborhood evangelism. Now we are going to look into the mechanics of starting and leading a group. These guidelines have come out of my own experiences and the experiences of many others. Each group should adapt them to fit its own individual needs, because groups, like people, are all different.

There are some guidelines all groups need to follow to be truly evangelistic. These show us some things we can do and they also keep us from doing other things. Certain methods may be legitimate for other ministries but not for small evangelistic Bible studies.

The following are basic guidelines. Everything we do correlates with these:

> A *Neighborhood Bible Study's*
> *Purpose* is Evangelistic
> *Content* is the Word
> *Method* is Servant Leadership

By setting the goal of evangelism as our purpose,

we naturally aim at introducing our neighbors to Jesus Christ as Saviour—the One who can take their burden of sin and give them joy and strength in its place.

By determining the content to be the Word of God, we limit our study to the Books in the Bible—especially those that will reveal Jesus and His message to them.

Because our method is servant leadership, we act as facilitators for the group. We try to serve the group by helping each member discover for herself the truths in God's Word.

Ingredients of a Bible Study

What is a neighborhood Bible study? Consider this definition:

A Neighborhood   Neighbors + Leader +
Bible Study = Time + Place + Acts 2:42

Neighbors

The number of neighbors involved in each group can be from three to twelve. When more than 12 people join a group it should be divided. Since the discussion method is used, full involvement of group members is hindered if the group is too large. The quiet ones retreat into silence, and by failing to contribute they also fail to discover and learn.

Leader

The leader is neither a lecturer nor a teacher, but rather a guide who asks questions. She keeps the group looking into the Word for the answers. She is not the authority in the discussion. The Word of God is the authority.

Leaderless groups do not exist. If one person is not recognized as the leader from the beginning, a leader will emerge from the group. This may not be the person most qualified for the position. It is best to have two Christians sharing the responsibility of a particular Bible study. One can assume leadership of the discussion, while the other serves as hostess. More will be said about their individual responsibilities later.

Time

A regular time must be set aside for the neighborhood Bible study. It is not a matter of meeting when convenient. The leader sets the example in faithfully committing herself to this segment of time. As the neighbors become involved, they will arrange their other activities around the weekly group meetings.

The leader should be careful about starting and stopping on time. If the meeting is scheduled to begin at 1 p.m. and end at 2:30 p.m., Christian courtesy and honesty demand that the wishes and obligations of the members be considered enough to work within these time limits. Carelessness in this can result in loss of members.

Place

Wherever it is convenient to meet is the place for a neighborhood Bible study. Groups most often meet in homes, but this does not exclude offices, restaurants, or wherever people get together.

When meeting in homes, rotate the meeting place if possible. This brings the members into a deeper commitment to the Bible study.

Acts 2:42

"And they continued steadfastly in the apostles'

doctrine and fellowship, and in breaking of bread, and in prayers."

A Biblical Pattern

This threefold pattern—the study of the Word, fellowship, and prayer—found in the Early Church becomes the pattern for a neighborhood Bible study.

Study of the Word

The study included at the end of this book, *Looking at Jesus With Luke*, is intended for beginning groups. We have used it successfully as an introduction to who Jesus is and why He came. It purposely consists of only six lessons. Non-Christians are willing to commit themselves if it is not for too long a period.

The guide for the Luke study presents questions that will help the group discuss what they read in the Scripture passage. The questions fall into the three categories of an inductive Bible study:

1. Observation—What does it say?
2. Interpretation—What does it mean?
3. Application—What does it mean to me?

Prayer

Jesus said that where two or three gather in His name, He will be there with them. Begin each session by recognizing His presence through prayer. This should be done in two or three simple and brief sentences.

Each study should also conclude with prayer. The conversational method—simply having a conversation with God—is best for neighborhood Bible studies. It draws the non-Christian as well as the Christian into a more direct confrontation with God.

The discussion method helps people to open their

hearts to the Word. Conversational prayer helps them to respond to the Spirit and prepares them for a miraculous renewal of life.

Fellowship

The fellowship within a group acts both as a bridge builder and as a door to caring.

The non-Christian neighbor coming into a Bible study needs to relate to something before she can relax and become involved. Refreshments and a time for casual conversation can accomplish this. When she gets to know you on a personal basis, you can introduce her to another Person, Jesus Christ.

Ten minutes over a cup of coffee before the Bible study begins and 20 minutes of fellowship afterwards builds friendships that strengthen the Christian's witness and makes the Bible study more inviting for the non-Christian.

How to Get Started

Now that we know what ingredients go into a neighborhood Bible study, where do we start?

Contact Your Pastor

Before starting a neighborhood Bible study, obtain your pastor's permission. It will not be necessary for him to attend the group, but you should keep him informed of your progress.

Your pastor's help will be valuable in answering questions raised by group members. He can also provide counseling to those in need, and you may want him to make pastoral calls on the sick or bereaved.

The ultimate goal of the neighborhood Bible study is that entire families will accept Jesus and be brought under the ministry of your pastor where they will continue to grow in the grace and knowledge of Jesus Christ. Involve him as your co-worker.

Identify Your Neighbors

With whom does God mean for you to share the gospel? God has put you in a particular neighborhood and in the company of certain people. Think about those with whom you spend time. Determine to build friendships with the non-Christians around you. For non-Christians to accept your invitation to a Bible study, you must have already won their confidence.

Jesus said we are to be the salt of the earth and the light of the world. To be useful as salt, we must move out into areas where salt is needed. To be seen as light, we must invade the darkness. To be witnesses to God's good news, we must make the acquaintance of those who are living in bondage to sin.

Pray for Your Neighborhood

When you enter into a witnessing ministry you engage in spiritual warfare. So you need to pray.

Pray that the Spirit of God will guide you and give you wisdom, discernment, and courage. Pray for a co-worker who will share the burden of the work with you.

The success of a neighborhood Bible study is in proportion to the amount of time spent in prayer interceding for your non-Christian neighbors. You will be interceding when you:

Pray for each individual neighbor by name.

Pray for insights into their needs.

Pray for normal contacts with them.

Pray that God will prepare them to receive your invitation to a neighborhood Bible study.

Remember, God answers specific prayers in specific ways.

Plan a Presentation

With the help of the person you have chosen as your co-worker plan a morning coffee hour or afternoon tea. Arrange for someone other than yourself or your co-worker to present a sample Bible lesson. After the study, ask your neighbors if they would be interested in continuing this study each week.

The reason for having someone else present this sample lesson is that in case your neighbors reject the idea of a Bible study, they can do so without rejecting you. This will make it easier for you to continue to live as a Christian witness among them.

Invite Your Neighbors

Invite all your neighbors. God did not give us the responsibility of prejudging who should receive the gospel and who should not. Some whom you think will not be interested may be the ones who will come. Inviting your neighbors is a step of faith—faith that God has put this ministry into your hands and that He has prepared your neighbors to respond.

People come for a variety of reasons. Some come for the social contact or intellectual enrichment, but many come because there is a spiritual hunger in their hearts. Whatever the reason, all will hear the teachings of God's Word. Some will nurture the seed of faith, while others will trample it out or let the cares of this world smother it. God has entrusted us with sowing and watering, but He has reserved the responsibility of the increase for himself.

An alternative idea for starting a neighborhood Bible study is to find two other Christians to join with you in this outreach. Pray together and plan a presentation as already described. Then each of you should invite two non-Christian friends who have never been in a Bible study before. There will be nine of you at the coffee or tea, with more non-Christians present than Christians. It is important to keep this balance.

Co-workers

Although some women lead a neighborhood Bible study without a co-worker, I have found it both helpful and encouraging to have someone work with me. One woman can take the responsibility of leading the discussion while the other acts as the hostess.

The hostess, as a co-worker, should be prepared to support the discussion leader in prayer and attitude. While the discussion is in progress the hostess should pray that the Lord's illuminating power will work in the hearts of the women and also that He'll give the leader wisdom as she guides the discussion. The hostess should be prepared and willing to enter into the discussion as the Lord leads, but wise enough to be quiet when others should be answering the questions.

The hostess is responsible for inviting friends and neighbors to the group. If women miss meetings the hostess should call during the week to let them know they were missed and to find out if there is any problem.

The physical preparations for the meetings are taken care of by the hostess. If the Bible study is conducted in her home, she will want to create an atmosphere conducive to studying the Word of God. The hostess takes charge of coffee and refreshments (which should always be done in moderation). She also arranges for the baby-sitting.

The leader and the hostess are the key persons in

any Bible study. They need to share the conviction that God has placed them with that particular group of women for that particular time. They also need to possess a willingness to be servants of others. As a team they will be used of God to introduce others to Jesus Christ.

The First Meeting

At the very first meeting certain things must happen to insure the neighbors' desire to return. The leader needs to arrive early so she is there to welcome the others as they arrive. Starting and stopping on time is most important and this is the leader's responsibility.

Enough Bible-study booklets should be available for everyone to have a copy.

It's important that the women have these to take home with them so they can spend time before the next meeting doing the lesson. This will get them into the Word during the week.

It is best to have copies of the New Testament in a modern translation. I recommend *Good News for Modern Man* because it is in modern English and is inexpensive. If everyone has the same translation the leader can ask the group to turn to a certain page number. Then nobody will be embarrassed because she doesn't know how to find the Book in the Bible.

The seating for the meeting should be arranged in a circle so everyone is facing each other. Looking at the back of someone's head discourages discussion. A comfortable temperature and enough ventilation are important factors in providing an inviting atmosphere.

During the meeting the leader sets the tone. It is her responsibility to see that everyone has an opportunity to talk. The way people interact at the first meeting sets a pattern for all succeeding meetings.

The leader is not the "answer man." She must anticipate questions but not answer them. Her job is to lead the women to discover for themselves what God's Word says and then to discuss it.

When the meeting is over, the leader should talk with every woman who has come. If possible, she should get some feedback on how they felt about the meeting.

An Agreement

A final word. Many problems will be solved before they occur if, at the very first meeting while discussing the possibility of having a neighborhood Bible study, you draw up a simple agreement. This can be done verbally, but the group needs to agree on the following:

> Purpose of the group
> Where and when the meetings will be held
> Maximum size of the group
> What Book in the Bible the group will study
> Who the leader is
> To limit the discussion to the portion of Scripture being studied
> Not to bring in denominational doctrines

An agreement such as this needs to be renewed for each new study begun. For example, when a group finishes the study of Luke, if it wishes to go on to study another Book, it should renew the agreement.

* * * * *

In the beginning of this book I quoted Jesus' words to His disciples in Matthew 9:37: "The harvest truly is plenteous, but the laborers are few."

Then I tried to show how plenteous the harvest is today. Verse 38 contains a command to be obeyed: "Pray ye therefore the Lord of the harvest, that he will send forth laborers into his harvest."

If you want to feel the heartbeat of God, become involved in the harvest. Pray for laborers and then go to your neighbors with the Bread of Life in your hands.

Looking at Jesus With Luke

How to Use This Study

Provide each group member with a copy of this study guide before the first meeting. (Available from Gospel Publishing House, 1445 Boonville, Springfield, MO 65802. Order No. 02-0756.) Lessons should be prepared at home before the meeting.

Read through the passages of Scripture before discussing them.

Ask the questions. Deal with each one as adequately as possible before proceeding to the next.

Encourage the members to share with the group the answers they have written in their books.

Allow time for and encourage discussion of the questions as they are presented. Do avoid tangents.

Make sure the answers come from the passage of Scripture being studied. The purpose of these studies is to find out what the Bible says, not what our church doctrines are.

At the end of an hour's study (an hour is long enough for any discussion) summarize what has been discussed, emphasizing the scriptural applications to our everyday lives.

1 Jesus Introduced

Luke 4:16-39

vv. 16-30

1. Retrace the steps of Jesus from the time He entered Nazareth until He left. Describe His actions. How did He enter Nazareth and how did He leave?

2. What do these actions reveal about Jesus' character?

3. What does the portion of Scripture He read tell us about Him? Summarize in your own words what He was saying He had come to accomplish.

4. What needs do people have today that could be met by any or all of these ministries?

5. What does the audience's reaction (v. 22) tell us about them? What attitude was behind their question about who Jesus was?

6. Why did this bother Jesus?

7. What do you think they understood Jesus to be saying to them in vv. 25-27?

Note: The widow Jesus referred to was living in a city in the Gentile country of Phoenicia. Naaman was a Gentile, a captain in the Syrian army.

8. In the context of this paragraph, who in God's sight are the poor, the captives, the blind, and the downtrodden of this world? Who are the ones who truly see and are free? Into which category did the people in the synagogue that day in Nazareth fall? Why?

___
___

vv. 31-39:

9. Retrace the sequence of events in these verses. How did each of these events bear witness to who Jesus is?

___
___

10. How did the response in Capernaum compare with that in Nazareth?

___
___

11. How do these responses to Jesus, in Nazareth and in Capernaum, compare with people's responses to Jesus today?

___
___

12. In this chapter, Luke is introducing us to Jesus as a public man. Who is he trying to tell us Jesus is?

___
___

13. From what we have observed, how important does our response to Jesus become?

___
___

14. From what we have learned in this chapter, what

needs do I have that Jesus can take care of? What has my response been to Jesus?

15. What can I learn from the response of Peter's mother-in-law that will help me when God does something for me?

2 Jesus Involved

Luke 5:1-26
vv. 1-11:

Note: "Lake Gennesaret" is another name for the Sea of Galilee.

1. Where have we met Simon before and under what circumstances? What had Simon already learned about Jesus?

2. Compare the two requests Jesus made of Simon in vv. 3, 4. In what way do they differ? What is Jesus asking of Simon in one request that He is not asking in the other?

3. What do you think Simon's feelings were about each request? Notice the progression of thought in Simon's answer in v. 5.

4. What are the two facts Simon learned from the experience? Compare how he addressed Jesus in vv. 5 and 8.

5. Why did Simon have to acknowledge both these facts before he could become a follower of Jesus?

vv. 12-16:

Note: "Leprosy and death were equally defiling according to Jewish law. Lepers were banished from all social contact, doomed to live with their own kind outside the city walls. They were to call, 'Unclean! Unclean!' so that others might avoid them and not be defiled. All must keep at least six feet from a leper, and if the wind came from his direction, a hundred feet was scarcely sufficient. This helps us appreciate the contrast between Jesus and all others. After all, he 'touched' the leper" (Rosalind Rinker, *Who Is This Man?* [Grand Rapids: Zondervan Publishing House, n.d.]).

6. What do the words of the leper to Jesus show us about his need? What characteristics are revealed in the leper?

7. How did Jesus' response answer that need?

8. What threefold command did Jesus give to the healed man? Why did He request these three things to be done?

9. In v. 15, what was the reaction of the community?

10. How did Jesus respond to this sudden fame? Why?

_____

_____

vv. 17-26:

11. What new types of people were now beginning to follow Jesus? These were the religious leaders. Why do you think they were showing up?

_____

12. Place yourself in that crowd. Describe the sequence of events and your feelings of the moment in vv. 18-20.

_____

13. What prompted Jesus to respond to the man's need? How did He respond?

_____

14. Who reacted to Jesus' statement? How did they interpret Jesus' statement to the paralytic? Why did they accuse Jesus of blasphemy?

_____

15. How did Jesus' answer in v. 23 and His action in v. 24 answer their accusation? (For the phrase "whether is easier, to say" substitute "which requires more authority.")

_____

16. How did the paralytic express his faith? Compare his response to that of the Pharisees.

_____

_____

17. How did the crowd react? To whom did the crowd give the credit for this miracle?

18. In these three incidents, Jesus revolutionized the lives of three very different men who each had his own unique need. How did they differ from each other in their life circumstances, as well as their needs? How did each one respond to Jesus' meeting his need? What was the one characteristic all three had in common in their response to Jesus?

19. What do these stories show me about Jesus' ability to meet my needs? Can I identify with any of these men and their basic needs?

Note: Peter's need was not to catch a boat load of fish, but to learn who Jesus was and who he was.

3 Jesus Teaching

Luke 6:20-49

A disciple is "one who accepts and assists in spreading the doctrine of another."

In this passage, Jesus is speaking directly to those

men He had just chosen to be His disciples. Much can be learned here about what it means to be a disciple.

vv. 20-26:

1. Make a chart showing who is blessed and how, who is pronounced judgment upon, and the reward of each:

    BLESSED ARE   REWARD

    WOE UNTO   REWARD

2. Put in your own words the contrast between the two groups of people, both in their present state and in the future.

   ___

3. Why would the disciples be hated and spoken of as evil? Who else was treated this way?

   ___

4. Who would be spoken well of?

   ___

vv. 27-38:

5. In vv. 27-30, Jesus gave certain commands that would serve to guide His disciples' responses to others, especially those who would mistreat them. List these commands. Then think of a real-life, contemporary situation in which each of these commands should be obeyed.

   ___

6. What basic rule does Jesus give in v. 31 to cover all situations? Put this in your own words.

7. What reasons does He give in vv. 32-34 for these responses He expected from His disciples?

8. What is the reward for obeying these commands?

9. Who is the example to be followed? How does He set an example? How has your own experience proved this to be true?

10. How do vv. 37, 38 relate to the preceding commandments?

11. What would happen in the world around us if we all obeyed these commandments at all times?

vv. 39-45:

12. What two things is Jesus trying to tell His disciples they need to do before they can help another person?

13. Where do good or evil actions originate? What does the "mouth speaking" have to do with it?

vv. 46-49:

14. According to v. 46, is it enough to call Jesus, "Lord"? Why or why not?

15. Describe the person who obeys Jesus. Describe the one who disobeys. What do the two have in common? Where do they part ways?

16. At this time in your life, with which one do you more closely identify?

17. This portion of Jesus' teaching was directed to men who were chosen to be His disciples. Jesus progressed from telling them to expect suffering and persecution in this world (vv. 20-26) to how they should act toward others (vv. 27-38) to examining their own hearts (vv. 39-45) to who is the true disciple of His (vv. 46-49). In view of the definition of the term *disciple* given at the beginning of this lesson, why did Jesus feel it necessary to give all this instruction? What does it mean to be a disciple of Jesus?

4 Jesus' Pattern for Prayer

Luke 11:1-13

> "The Lord is nigh unto them that call upon him, to all that call upon him in truth" (Psalm 145:18)

vv. 1-4:

1. What do we learn about God from these verses?

2. What does it mean to pray, "Hallowed be thy name"?

3. On the basis of what we learn about God, what should our attitude be toward Him when we pray?

4. Why do we need to pray, "Thy kingdom come"?

5. Put in your own words, "Thy will be done, as in heaven, so in earth." What difference would this prayer make in the world around us if it were sincerely prayed? What difference would it make in your own personal life?

6. What areas of our lives are covered by the next three petitions?

7. How can we who live in comparative prosperity pray sincerely, "Give us . . . our daily bread"?

8. Why do you think Jesus attached a "condition-to-be-met" on the petition for forgiveness? What does an unforgiving attitude do to us personally—psychologically, physically, and spiritually?

9. Explain in your own words why the last petition is important.

vv. 5-13:

10. In this parable, what is Jesus trying to show us about the nature of prayer?

11. How important is it to be specific when we pray?

12. What attributes of God does Jesus reveal in this parable?

13. Why does Jesus bring in the gift of the Holy Spirit here in His teaching on prayer? How does the Holy Spirit help us?

14. In both of these parables, what assurance does Jesus present to those who pray?

Review the Lord's Prayer. List briefly in Column 1 the petitions in the order Jesus gave them. In Column 2, write your own personal petitions that relate to each of those in Column 1:

COLUMN 1   COLUMN 2

5 Jesus Crucified

A number of times throughout His ministry, Jesus told His disciples He was going to be crucified. "The Son of Man must suffer many things, and be rejected by the elders and chief priests and scribes, and be killed, and be raised up on the third day" (Luke 9:22, *NASB*). His purpose in coming to earth was to die and be raised again. This study and the next one explores this purpose and how it relates to our lives.

Luke 23:33-56

vv. 33-38:

1. How was the suffering of Jesus different from that of the two thieves?

2. Contrast in your own words the actions of the soldiers on the ground and what was happening above them on the cross. How is this symbolic of the human dilemma?

3. Who had the last word on the description of Jesus that was placed over the cross? (See John 19:19-22.)

vv. 39-43:

4. What did the two criminals both acknowledge about Jesus? How did each respond to his understanding of who Jesus was?

   _____

5. How are these two reactions similar to human responses today?

   _____

vv. 44-49:

6. Describe the events of these verses in the order in which they happened.

   _____

7. Contrast the reaction of the centurion with that of the multitude. What did each show about their understanding of the events?

   _____

8. In vv. 33-46, Jesus made three statements from the cross. What do these tell us about Him?

   _____

9. How was His death a triumph? Who was in control of His death?

   _____

vv. 50-56:

10. Who was Joseph? What kind of man was he? What quality in Joseph did the death of Jesus bring out?

    _____

11. What does the action of the women show about their understanding of the Crucifixion?

Read Isaiah 53:

12. Isaiah wrote this prophecy under the inspiration of the Holy Spirit hundreds of years before Christ's death. Observe the details that parallel the details of Jesus' death. What does Isaiah tell us is the purpose of Jesus' death? For whom did Jesus die? Why?

13. Isaiah 53 is a beautiful piece of poetry but the words became a reality in Jesus' life. How can they become a reality in your life?

6 Jesus Resurrected

Luke 24

vv. 1-12:

1. Why were the women going to the tomb? What did they find?

2. What was the message of the angels to the women? Of what did they remind the women? What was the women's response?

3. Why didn't the disciples believe the women's story?

Note: The *NASB* says, "They would not believe them" (v. 11). This indicates they willed not to believe.

4. Why did Peter run to the tomb? What did he find there?

vv. 13-35:

5. What were the two men walking to Emmaus talking about? What was their general attitude?

6. Why did they not recognize Jesus?

7. How did they describe Jesus? What had they expected Him to do? What had the women told them that disturbed them?

8. For what did Jesus rebuke them?

9. Why did Jesus lead them in a review of the Scriptures? Why was this important to their recognition of Him?

10. Why did they urge Jesus to stay with them?

11. What caused them to recognize Jesus?

12. What was their immediate reaction?

vv. 36-53:

13. Why were the disciples startled?

14. What proof did Jesus offer the disciples to show it was really Him and not a spirit?

15. Describe their reaction.

16. What further proof did Jesus give of His identity?

17. What did Jesus do for them personally? Why was it important for them to understand the Scriptures?

18. What message did He tell the disciples would be preached? Where would it start? Who would preach it?

19. What promise did He give them? What were the instructions He gave that they might receive the promise?

20. Where did the disciples go when Jesus left them? What was their attitude? How could they be so bold and joyful in the temple where the priests were who had put Jesus to death?

21. Luke gives three incidents related to the resurrection of Jesus: The women at the empty tomb; the two disciples conversing with Jesus on the way to Emmaus, and the 11 disciples gathered together.

   Describe the difference in the disciples' attitudes before and after each appearance of Jesus. Their actions? What difference should the Resurrection make in our lives today?

Resource Materials

Guides for Group Study

Fromer, Margaret, and Sharrel Keyes. *Let's Pray Together: Eight Studies on Prayer*. Wheaton, IL: Harold Shaw Publishers, 1974.

Hunt, Gladys M. *Eyewitness: John's View of Jesus*. Wheaton, IL: Harold Shaw Publishers, 1971.

Hunt, Gladys M. *The God Who Understands Me: Studies in the Sermon on the Mount*. Wheaton, IL: Harold Shaw Publishers, 1971.

Kunz, Marilyn, and Catherine Schell. *Neighborhood Bible Studies Series* (includes the books listed below). Wheaton, IL: Tyndale House Publishers: *Mark*; *Conversations With Jesus*; *Acts*; *Romans*; *1 John and James*; *They Met Jesus*; and *Psalms and Proverbs*.

How to Start and Lead a Small-group Bible Study

Burnham, David, and Sue Burnham. *A Bible Study in My House?* Chicago: Moody Press, 1975.

Hunt, Gladys M. *It's Alive: The Dynamics of Small Group Studies*. Wheaton, IL: Harold Shaw Publishers, 1971.

Kunz, Marilyn, and Catherine Schell. *How to Start a*

Bible Study. Wheaton, IL: Tyndale House Publishers, 1966.

Wollen, Albert J. *Miracle of Group Bible Study.* Glendale, CA: Gospel Light Publications, 1976.

Background Reading for Group Leaders

Bennett, Dennis, and Rita Bennett. *The Holy Spirit and You.* Plainfield, NJ: Logos International, 1971.

Lewis, Clive S. *Mere Christianity.* New York: MacMillan Publishing Co., 1964.

Lewis, Clive S. *Miracles: A Preliminary Study.* New York: MacMillan Publishing Co., 1963.

Little, Paul E. *How to Give Away Your Faith.* Downers Grove, IL: InterVarsity Press, 1966.

Little, Paul E. *Know Why You Believe.* Downers Grove, IL: InterVarsity Press, rev. ed., 1968.

Rinker, Rosalind. *Prayer: Conversing With God.* Grand Rapids: Zondervan Publishing House, n.d.

Sherrill, John L. *They Speak With Other Tongues.* Old Tappan, NJ: Revell, 1965.

Notes

Notes

Notes

Notes